Great
WINE TOURS
OF THE WORLD

Great
WINE TOURS
OF THE WORLD

GENERAL EDITOR
JIM BUDD

BARNES
&NOBLE
BOOKS
NEW YORK

This edition published by Barnes & Noble, Inc.,
by arrangement with New Holland Publishers (U.K.) Ltd.

2003 Barnes & Noble Books

M 10 9 8 7 6 5 4 3 2 1

ISBN 0 7607 4209 X

Although the publishers have made every effort to ensure that the information
contained in this book was meticulously researched and correct at the time of going to
press, they accept no responsibility for any inaccuracies, loss, injury, or inconvenience
sustained by any person using this book as reference.

Publisher: Mariëlle Renssen
Commissioning editor: Mari Roberts
Managing editors: Claudia dos Santos, Simon Pooley
Managing art editor: Richard MacArthur
Editor: Gill Gordon
Designer: Christelle Marais
Cartographer: Carl Germishuys
Picture researcher: Karla Kik
Proofreader/Indexer: Ingrid Corbett
Production: Myrna Collins

Reproduction by Hirt & Carter (Pty) Ltd, Cape Town
Printed and bound in Singapore by Tien Wah Press (Pte) Ltd

HALF TITLE PAGE A brisk stroll through the vineyards of the Rauenthaler Berg, in the
Rheingau, on a misty fall morning, is the best way to prepare for a day's touring.
TITLE PAGE Situated near Calistoga in Napa, California, the vaulted cellar at Clos Pegase
forms an elegant setting for winery dinners. The estate also has a notable art collection.
RIGHT At Château de Rully, a top property in Burgundy's Côte Chalonnaise, the wine is
made and sold by Antonin Rodet, one of the region's most quality-conscious companies.
CONTENTS PAGE Evening view from Bodegas Castillo de Monjardín, Navarra, Spain.
Earthenware jars, like those in the foreground, known as *tinajas*, were used a century ago
both for fermenting and storing wine; things are very different today.

CONTENTS

GENERAL
INTRODUCTION

JIM BUDD

Wine reflects both the place where it was made and the people who made it. Meeting the producer and seeing the place where a particular wine was grown and made adds an extra dimension to enjoying it. There is something very magical about visiting a vineyard in the company of a winemaker who is passionate about the wine he or she produces. Then later, tasting those wines, perhaps in an old cellar hewn out of rock, or in a modern tasting room, with the winemaker talking you through how the wines were made, before enjoying the same wines during a long and leisurely lunch, probably outside, and perhaps with a view of vine-clad hillsides. Wine touring is a wonderful blend of learning and pleasure.

Vines tend to produce their best fruit when they are planted on slopes with thin, barely fertile soil where they have best exposure to the sun and get limited water. Sometimes the slopes are gentle, as in Burgundy's Côte d'Or or Australia's McLaren Vale. Sometimes they are spectacularly steep, as in Portugal's Douro or Germany's Mosel.

Many wine regions are startlingly beautiful, so it is little wonder that wine lovers want to visit them. Wine tourism, however, is a new phenomenon that has arisen over the last 30 years. In part, this reflects the huge growth of travel in the latter half of the 20th century, but also that wine regions, and those who make wine, are now seen as interesting to visit. A dramatic expansion in the number of countries producing and exporting quality wine has helped generate interest.

This has not always been the case. In the early part of the 20th century it was unusual for wine merchants in the UK, an almost non-wine-producing country at the center of the wine trade, to travel to the wine regions to discover new producers and taste new wines. Certainly there were some merchants who served apprenticeships in the classic regions such as Bordeaux, Jerez and Oporto, but this was as far as they traveled. In 1934 Charles Edward Berry of Berry Bros & Rudd, London's oldest wine merchant, published a diary of an eight-week pioneering journey he made around the wine regions of France.

In contrast however, over the last few decades, there has been an enormous change in world wine consumption. Wine drinking has risen in non-wine-producing countries and fallen in wine-producing ones. Everywhere, there has been a move towards drinking higher quality wines, even if there are fears in some quarters that wines are beginning to taste the same, irrespective of where they come from. Understandably, many consumers have become increasingly curious about the wines they are drinking, wanting to know what grape varieties are used, who made them, and where exactly they come from.

In many ways, visiting small producers is a lot more fun than visiting large wineries, but it also involves more preparation. Naturally the chances of meeting Robert, Michael, or Tim Mondavi if you visit their Oakville winery in Napa are slim indeed. However, the visitor facilities are extensive and very professionally set up. Visit a small producer, though, and there is a good chance that you will meet the winemaker, but you should always make an appointment in advance.

Small-scale producers frequently combine a whole host of roles: looking after the vineyards, making the wine, selling it, keeping the accounts, as well as receiving visitors. So do not be surprised if the key people are not there if you turn up without warning. Larger wineries often employ staff specifically to welcome visitors, especially during peak periods, so advance notice may not be necessary.

THIS PAGE (LEFT TO RIGHT) Poppies, wheat and vines are typical of much of the French countryside, as here at Souzay, Maine-et-Loire; vine-clad terraces line the hillsides at Quinta do Noval in Pinhão, Douro; golden sun-kissed vines are reflected in Lake Dunstan, near Bannockburn, Central Otago, New Zealand; at Pine Ridge winery in Napa, as throughout the wine world, roses are not just an attractive feature, they serve as an early indicator of vineyard pests and diseases. PREVIOUS PAGES Autumnal vineyards surround Niedermorschwihr, near Colmar, Alsace. The steep Sommerberg grand cru (left), is known for its riesling.

Worldwide there are an increasing number of companies that organize tours of wine regions. The advantage is that these companies will make all the arrangements for you and have the sort of contacts that enable them to organize introductions and meetings with producers that would be impossible for an individual visitor to manage. On the other hand you will be traveling with a group of strangers, who may or may not be to your liking.

Organized trips also have the advantage that someone else is doing the driving, so there is no need to worry about directions, or about drinking and driving. Limits on how much you can drink and still drive a car legally are increasingly strict worldwide and often rigorously enforced. It is not unknown in France to be stopped for a roadside alcohol check by a soldier carrying a sub-machine gun! Wine tasting is not a recognized legal defense. If you are doing the driving, you should certainly be spitting out your wine during a tasting.

Many people think that spitting out wine during a tasting is a waste. But there is a difference between wine tasting and wine drinking, especially if you are wanting to carefully evaluate wines, perhaps to decide whether you want to buy them. Alcohol soon clouds one's judgment, which, of course, is why it is so popular. Most tasting rooms now provide something to spit into. Occasionally, at the end of a tasting, a producer will open a special bottle – perhaps an old wine or a limited release. Then, of course, it might well be rude to spit this out.

Although many wine producers are very hospitable – the wine trade seems to attract an above average number of generous, friendly and interesting people – there are limits. Try to avoid turning up at lunchtime in France or Italy, for example, where the midday is still sacred. Obviously this is a different matter if there is a special tasting room or visitor center which is open all day. Don't forget that although you are on holiday, the producers are not. Should you buy some wine when you visit a producer? Some places charge for visits and tasting. Here, there is no reason why you should feel obliged to buy any wine unless you wish to. If, however, there is no charge and a producer spends time with you, opening bottles, it is only right that you should buy some wine at the end of your visit. It is clearly unreasonable to spend an hour with a producer and leave with only a word of thanks.

With so many fascinating places to visit, it is impossible to cover them all, and a mix of well-known and lesser-known regions have been selected. Champagne, for instance, has not been included because it is so well-known. The Right Bank of Bordeaux was chosen because the landscape around St-Emilion is much more attractive than the low-lying land of the Médoc, while in Australia, the McLaren Vale and Margaret River regions are featured rather than the better known Barossa.

Wine is made to be enjoyed. Whether you acquired it on your travels or bought it locally, a special bottle opened at home can remind you of the places you saw, the people you met, and the pleasure you had when visiting the region where it was made.

RIGHT Jacques Seysses of Domaine Dujac watches his pruning team work in the Clos de la Roche vineyard on a cold December morning, Morey-St-Denis, Côte d'Or, France.

INTRODUCTION

THE OLD WORLD
THE CLASSIC REGIONS OF EUROPE

JIM BUDD

Back in the 1960s, the classic regions of Europe – Bordeaux, Burgundy, Champagne, the Douro, Jerez, Mosel, Piedmont, Rheingau, the Rhône and possibly a few isolated producers in Tuscany – were the only ones producing wines of significant quality. However, over the past 40-plus years, the face of wine has changed utterly. There have been huge technological changes, especially the advent of temperature control, and today we understand the process of making wine very much better than we used to. This greater knowledge gives winemakers greater control, with far fewer faulty wines being made now than was the case in the past. Today, high-quality wine is produced all over the world and sold into a global market.

Over the last decades it has been convenient to divide the wine world into two: the Old and the New World. Of late that distinction has become increasingly blurred. There is an enormous, and ongoing, exchange of ideas and knowledge between the various wine areas. Burgundian producers go to New Zealand to make the vintage and vice versa. Wine consultants, like France's Michel Rolland, travel all over the world to give advice. A new generation of 'flying winemaker' works two harvests a year, shuttling back and forth between 'old' and 'new' worlds with consummate ease. There are more and more joint ventures between wine companies based, for example, in Australia and Chile, Italy and the USA, France and Argentina ... the list is endless.

The classic grape varieties, in particular cabernet sauvignon, merlot and sauvignon blanc from Bordeaux, and chardonnay and pinot noir from Burgundy, have been planted in countries outside Europe, transforming their wines. Many parts of Europe, in particular southern France, southern Italy, and Sicily, which previously produced 'plonk,' are increasingly making quality wines which are arguably more New than Old World.

Even so there are still very significant differences between the classic wines of Europe and those of the rest of the world. Europe has a much longer tradition of wine production, which began in the regions around the Mediterranean and dates to the times of the ancient Greeks and Romans. Traveling around European vineyards, it is not unusual to meet producers whose families have been making wine from the same plots of land for a number of generations. Some go even further: the leading Italian producer, Antinori, for example, can trace an involvement in wine going back 600 years.

For the wine enthusiast, there are areas and vineyard sites which are thrilling to visit because they are so famous and have such a long tradition. The roll call of famous names down Burgundy's Côte d'Or is one such instance. There is a certain magic in looking at the small plots of land that make up Montrachet or Romanée-Conti, even if the chances for most of us of being able to afford their wines are slim.

There are also a greater number of family-run vineyards in Europe than elsewhere, with the inherent respect for tradition and continuity that this provides. The average-sized property in France is only 12 acres (five hectares). In contrast over 80 percent of Australia's wine is made by just four companies, while in Chile there are estates with over 4840 acres (2000 hectares) of vines. In the Old World, individual attention can be lavished on vines and wine making in a way that large-scale New World producers can never achieve.

Partly to meet the challenge from the rest of the world, and partly in an attempt to woo new customers in the face of competition, many European producers and regions are making dramatic improvements in quality. Many have opened their cellar doors and now welcome visitors, where previously their wines could only be obtained through merchants or retail outlets. This is an exciting time to visit them.

LEFT A view that is not for the faint-hearted! Vertiginous vineyards look down on the imposing Scharzhof winery, part of the Egon Muller estate, at the foot of Scharzhof Berg, in the Saar, Mosel. Steep-sided valleys are typical of this area, making viticulture something of a challenge.

PREVIOUS PAGES During the Middle Ages, the town of St-Emilion played an important part in shipping wine down the Dordogne River. Situated on the route the pilgrims took to reach Santiago de Compostela in northern Spain, its tradition of hospitality continues to be evident in its modern role as a favorite tourism destination.

BORDEAUX

ST-EMILION, POMEROL & FRONSAC

JAMES LAWTHER MW

The Garonne and Dordogne rivers run like arteries through the Bordeaux landscape, flowing downstream into the Atlantic Ocean. West of the Garonne are the left bank vineyards of the Médoc and Graves. East of the Dordogne is the Libournais, the right bank sector of St-Emilion, Pomerol and Fronsac. This is Bordeaux's most historic wine region and, with its rolling countryside, one of the most picturesque. It is also a region buzzing with renewed vigor as producers benefit from a rekindled notoriety and prosperity.

Viticulture on the right bank can be traced back to Gallo-Roman times and the names of some of the great estates hark back to this period: Château Ausone from the poet Ausonius, and Figeac from the original proprietor. In the Middle Ages, when the area formed part of the English fief of Aquitaine, a healthy trade in wine was established across the English Channel. The town council, or jurade, whose powers were granted by England's King John in 1199, governed the wine business from St-Emilion. The walled town of Libourne was founded in 1270 to control river traffic down the Dordogne. The church remained the major landowner until the French Revolution, as witnessed by the number of religious ruins. The land was farmed as small units under a system of share-cropping, and today the majority of estates continue as small, family-run affairs, with the average holding just 12–20 acres (5–8 hectares).

The name St-Emilion has always been a magic draw. In the past, wines from a region that extended as far as Bergerac bore the title St-Emilionnais or Près St-Emilion. Only with the instigation of *appellation contrôlée* in 1935 were the boundaries clearly drawn. St-Emilion was delimited to the nine parishes listed in the original King John Charter of 1199, while the

LEFT The medieval town of St-Emilion huddles in a cleft of limestone hills, with the 13th-century King's Tower, at left, and the bell tower of the monolithic church illuminated by the late evening light.

satellite communes of Lussac, Montagne, Puisseguin and St-Georges were allowed to append the St-Emilion handle to their names, and Pomerol and Fronsac were recognized as individual appellations.

The beautiful medieval town of St-Emilion with its cobbled streets, terracotta-tiled houses, and sweeping views over the Dordogne Valley is the perfect base for exploring the region. It is also a focal point for gastronomy, so stop here and spend a few days touring the surrounding countryside.

Much of the architecture, including the imposing church and 13th-century King's Tower, is constructed from stone quarried from the surrounding limestone plateau, giving a warm glow to the exteriors and providing a warren of underground galleries for cellaring wine. The whole vineyard zone, some 13,300 acres (5400 hectares), is such a cultural attraction it was declared a world heritage site by UNESCO (United Nations Educational, Scientific and Cultural Organization) in 1999.

Producers on the right bank are usually happy to receive visitors, but the rule of thumb to gain entry is always to make a prior appointment. This particularly applies to Pomerol where only 25 percent of producers live on the estate. The local *syndicats* and St-Emilion tourist office can help in this respect.

The right bank is essentially a red wine region, with only an anecdotal production of dry white. Merlot is the red grape variety, with a supporting cast of cabernet franc and, to a more limited degree, cabernet sauvignon. The essentially cool clay-limestone soils suit the earlier ripening merlot better than cabernet, providing wines that are full-bodied and generous, with the capacity to age. However, variations in the terroir produce subtle differences throughout the region, as do the permutations in the blend.

RIGHT AND BELOW Château Pétrus in Pomerol; an unprepossessing property which produces one of the world's most sought-after and expensive wines. At harvest time, the *hotte* carriers empty merlot grapes into a trailer under the watchful eye of proprietor Christian Mouiex.

OPPOSITE Situated on the outskirts of St-Emilion, the exceptional vineyard of Château Ausone faces east-southeast and is sheltered from wind, frost and hail. This Premier Grand Cru Classé estate dates to the 18th century.

The St-Emilion classification, which was instigated in 1955, is reviewed every 10 years. The last review took place in 1996 when 13 châteaux were designated Premier Grand Cru Classé. Of these, 11 are on the perimeter of the town of St-Emilion, so why not start the tour with a visit to one of these. Châteaux Belair and Clos Fourtet both have substantial underground cellars quarried from limestone.

Heading west towards Libourne the road runs down the hill through the Côtes and Pieds de Côtes where erosion has modified the clay-limestone soils. A patchwork quilt of vineyards, farmhouses and country lanes denotes the rural character of the region.

Turning towards Pomerol, the vineyards of two of St-Emilion's Premiers Grands Crus Classés, Château Figeac and Château Cheval Blanc, are located on either side of the road. A series of undulating gravel mounds runs northeast from Figeac's 18th-century château through Cheval Blanc and beyond. The sandy and gravelly soils here are similar to those found in the Médoc, which explains the higher percentage of cabernet sauvignon and cabernet franc found in these wines.

Looping east again towards Montagne, the road dips down and crosses the Barbanne River, really just a stream, the boundary delimiting St-Emilion from the satellite appellations of Montagne and St-Georges. Winding back up the hill, the aristocratic 18th-century Château St-Georges sits on a limestone promontory looking back at St-Emilion, while at Montagne there is a small wine museum, the Ecomusée du Libournais.

LEFT Vieux Château Certan, which is located at the heart of the Pomerol plateau, produces long-aging wines of great finesse.

On the outskirts of Puisseguin you'll find Les Producteurs Réunis, a cooperative which accounts for 20 percent of Puisseguin's production and 40 percent of Lussac's.

Continuing east, the road climbs to St-Philippe d'Aiguilhe, the highest point in the Gironde at 384 feet (117 meters), and one of the nine communes in the Côtes de Castillon, an appellation created in 1989 and still undergoing change. The wines are similar in style to St-Emilion and competitive in terms of value for money. Château d'Aiguilhe, with its ruined 13th-century château, is one of the top estates. If time allows, head for Castillon-la-Bataille where there is a great Monday food market, before returning to St-Emilion.

The second day can be devoted to visiting Pomerol and Fronsac. Take the road west again past Château Cheval Blanc and head straight on into Pomerol. The land appears flat with only the spire of Pomerol's church as a landmark. The properties look modest but don't let this fool you – some of the greatest and most expensive wines in the world are produced here. This is the central core of Pomerol, a plateau with a mix of clay and gravel soils, which produces wines of great opulence. The major estates are all gathered in this area: la Conseillante, l'Evangile, Vieux Château Certan, Trotanoy, and Pétrus. Even here the grandiose architecture is missing.

Further west the land slopes gently towards the tree-lined N89. Here, the soils are sandier and the wines lighter in style. Château de Sales is the largest estate in the 1940-acre (785-hectare) Pomerol appellation and has a château to match. To the north, the Barbanne River forms a boundary with Lalande de Pomerol. Crossing to the village of Néac the countryside becomes more undulating and the wines more similar in style to Pomerol, although with a little less weight and finesse.

Getting to Fronsac means skirting the northern fringes of the town of Libourne and heading across the Isle River. In contrast to Pomerol, this is a region of hills, or *tertres,* and plateaus. The wines, which are merlot-based and firmly structured, had a reputation to equal those of St-Emilion in the 18th-century and today they are making something of a comeback. The Maison des Vins in Fronsac offers a broad selection from local producers. Otherwise head into the back country around the village of Saillans where there are a number of excellent producers like Châteaux Dalem, Moulin-Haut-Laroque, Villars, and La Vieille Cure.

Visting the right bank can be either super-charged, or leisurely, as everything is relatively close to hand. It really depends on the number of châteaux you want to visit in a day. For the more energetic visitor, both the suggested circuits can be tackled by bicycle, which is a great way to see and feel the region (bicycles can be hired from the tourist office in St-Emilion). Buy your own food and picnic along the way or opt for a snack at one of the village cafés, reserving any gastronomic experience for the evening in St-Emilion. Local cuisine that features foie gras, duck, and entrecôte steak should quell even the most ravenous appetites.

MAIN GRAPES
Red: Merlot, cabernet franc, cabernet sauvignon.

LEADING WINES (APPELLATIONS)
St-Emilion, St-Emilion Grand Cru, Pomerol, Fronsac, Canon-Fronsac, Lalande de Pomerol, St-Emilion satellites (Montagne, Lussac, Puisseguin, St-Georges), Côtes de Castillon, Bordeaux-Côtes de Francs.

MAIN PRODUCERS
St-Emilion: Ch Ausone, Ch Cheval Blanc, Ch Figeac (*all 1er Grand Cru Classé*).
Pomerol: Ch Pétrus, Vieux Château Certan.
Fronsac: Ch La Vieille Cure.
Lalande de Pomerol: Ch La Fleur de Boüard.
St-Georges St-Emilion: Ch St-Georges.
Côtes de Castillon: Ch d'Aiguilhe.

MAIN TOWNS Bordeaux, Libourne.

AIRPORT AND TRAIN Mérignac-Bordeaux Airport. Bordeaux and Libourne are both served by the TGV (*train à grand vitesse*) high-speed rail link from Paris.

DAYS Two.

BEST TIME TO GO April to October.

LEFT Cèpe mushrooms are an autumnal specialty of the region.
CENTER Cave de l'Ermitage is one of a plethora of wine shops and cellars that nestle in the shadow of St-Emilion's famous bell tower.
RIGHT Members of St-Emilion's *confrèrie*, the Jurade, in procession to celebrate the *Ban des Vendanges*, or official opening of the harvest.

SUMMARY Day 1: St-Emilion – Montagne – Puisseguin – St-Philippe d'Aiguilhe – Castillon-la-Bataille – St-Emilion.
Day 2: St-Emilion – Pomerol – Néac – Libourne – Fronsac – Saillans – St-Emilion.

SOURCES OF INFORMATION
• *Office de Tourisme de St-Emilion*
Tel: +33 05.57.55.28.28.
Web: www.saint-emilion-tourisme.com
• *Maison du Vin de St-Emilion*
Tel: +33 05.57.55.50.55
Fax: +33 05.57.55.53.10.
• *Syndicat Viticole de Pomerol*
Tel: +33 05.57.25.06.88
Fax: +33 05.57.25.07.17.
• *Syndicat Viticole des Côtes de Castillon*
Tel: +33 05.57.40.00.88
Fax: +33 05.57.40.06.31.
• *Maison des Vins de Fronsac*
Tel: +33 05.57.51.80.51
Fax: +33 05.57.25.98.19.

BURGUNDY

STEPHEN BROOK

Burgundy is one of the ancient wine regions of France, and the broad outlines of its vineyards have scarcely altered in a thousand years. It was renowned for its wines in medieval times, and many of the great buildings belonging to the monasteries that once owned the vineyards are still standing. The landscape has changed so little because the location of the vineyards is determined by a precarious microclimate. Vines will thrive on a particular slope, but 150 feet higher it will be too cold for grapes to ripen properly. Broadly speaking, the vineyards line the east-facing slopes that stretch from Dijon in the north to well beyond Beaune to the south.

For many decades only two grape varieties have been cultivated here: chardonnay and pinot noir. It's true that there are a few exceptions: a little pinot gris or pinot blanc in the north, some aligoté and gamay in the south, but they are relatively insignificant. However, if the issue of grape variety is a simple one in Burgundy, everything else is fairly complicated!

The vineyards here are classified on a hierarchical basis which is quite easy to understand. Wines from the very best and most consistent sites are labeled as Grand Cru. These tend to be the most revered, and often most expensive, wines of Burgundy. Superior vineyards, much greater in number and acreage, are known as Premier Cru. All other vineyards within a particular village are only entitled to the village name, such as Volnay or Meursault. Those vineyards not within a specific village may only produce simple Bourgogne Rouge or Bourgogne Blanc.

This hierarchical system leads one to expect that the higher rated the vineyard, the better its wine will be. That's true in theory, but ignores the fact that a bad winemaker can let down the promise of an outstanding site. So in Burgundy it is important to know not only which are the best vineyards, but also who the best winemakers are. Inevitably, they are the ones who not only vinify skillfully, but who tend their vineyards carefully.

LEFT The pinot noir vineyards that encircle the village of Chambolle-Musigny yield some of the most exquisite and perfumed wines of the Côte de Nuits.

Pinot noir and chardonnay grapes are sensitive to yields, so the lower the crop the more intense the resulting wine is likely to be. Reducing yields means less wine available for sale, so many growers are reluctant to do it. Pinot noir is a fragile grape, with delicate red-fruit aromas, so nuances are all-important. Skillful winemakers will vary their techniques from vintage to vintage, taking care to express the exquisite fruitiness and scent of the grape, while at the same time trying to give the wine sufficient structure and balance to age well.

Visiting the vineyards of Burgundy is not that difficult. Beginning in the north, it is a slow trudge through the suburbs of Dijon to the wine villages of the Côte de Nuits which, with the more southerly Côte de Beaune, make up the region known as the Côte d'Or.

Marsannay, the first important village, is followed by the great names of the Côte de Nuits; Fixin, Gevrey-Chambertin, Morey-St-Denis, Chambolle-Musigny, Vougeot, Vosne-Romanée and Nuits-St-Georges.

You can take the main route, the busy N74, turning off from time to time to visit the villages and vineyards. But it's much more interesting, although slower, to drive through the vineyards themselves. A special *Route des Grands Crus* passes alongside some of Burgundy's most celebrated vineyards between Gevrey-Chambertin and Morey-St-Denis. Many vineyards are identified with a plaque or inscribed gateway, so equip yourself with a vineyard map if you want to pay homage to famous sites such as Corton-Charlemagne, Richebourg or Chambertin.

Beyond Nuits-St-Georges, the N74 passes through a region of quarries, where you can easily see the limestone soil that many believe explains the elegance of Burgundian wines.

Then you come to Ladoix, Aloxe-Corton and Savigny, all villages within the Côte de Beaune. The heart of this region is Beaune itself. Dijon has some worthwhile sites, notably the palace of the dukes of Burgundy, but the walled city of Beaune has much more charm. There is ample free parking close to the walls, so abandon your car and walk the short distance into the center. Beaune is an essential stopping-place. Most of the large wine merchants are based here and many of them are open to the public. For a modest fee, you can visit vaulted medieval cellars, learn about the region and its wines, and be rewarded with a tasting of a few wines. The town center is full of wine shops, so it's easy to stock up, although prices can be quite high. An unmissable tourist attraction is the beautiful medieval hospital known as the Hospices de Beaune, the site of an annual charity wine auction. Beaune is full of restaurants, and it is hard to eat badly here.

Going south from the city, you continue to traverse the Côte de Beaune, passing the villages of Pommard and Volnay on your right. Volnay soon merges with Meursault and, from this point, you are in chardonnay country. Above their eponymous villages, the famous vineyards of Meursault, Puligny-Montrachet and Chassagne-Montrachet all blend into one another.

Continuing south, beyond the little town of Chagny you enter the Côte Chalonnaise. Here the vineyards are more dispersed and are gathered around the principal villages of the region: Mercurey, Rully, Givry, Montagny. The wines are still authentic burgundies, but they can be a touch more rustic than those of the Côte d'Or; they are also considerably cheaper which, given the prices demanded for top burgundy, is an important factor.

RIGHT The village of Pernand-Vergelesses lies at the foot of the hill of Corton. The Grand Cru, Corton-Charlemagne, is grown on the west-facing slopes.
OPPOSITE With few properties in Vosne-Romanée open to visitors, the Maison des Vins in the village provides an opportunity to taste and buy wines.

With the average vineyard holding being around 15 acres (6 hectares) per proprietor, there are thousands of mostly small estates in Burgundy, and visiting them is not always easy. It is simple to visit the merchant houses in Beaune or Nuits St Georges but, by and large, they do not produce the best wines. On the other hand, the top domaines (estates) can sell their production 20 times over, and have no need to court visitors. Don't even attempt to visit, for example, the top-rated Domaine de la Romanée-Conti.

However, if you do have a favorite Burgundy producer, it is worth phoning in advance to make an appointment. If the producer has time to receive you, you can look forward to an interesting experience. Because a domaine may only produce a few thousand cases of wine a year, do not expect the owner to open a wide selection of bottles just for you. You will almost certainly be taken to the cellar though, where he will siphon wine into a glass directly from the barrel. That way you can compare the wines he makes from his various vineyards. It's fascinating to compare and contrast! You may find yourself invited to taste some bottled wines too, but don't count on it. You should not feel obliged to buy wine at the end of your visit, although an order for a few bottles will no doubt be appreciated.

New World-style tasting rooms are rare in Burgundy, but they do exist. You won't find them in the most fashionable villages such as Vosne-Romanée, but you will find them elsewhere. In Mercurey, for example, there is one at the excellent estate of Michel Juillot.

LEFT Le Montrachet, shared by the villages of Puligny-Montrachet and Chassagne-Montrachet, is Burgundy's most famous white wine vineyard.

BELOW LEFT This small wine shop is typical of the dozens that trade in Beaune. Not all of them offer wines of good quality or from good producers.

The adventurous wine tourist should look at off-the-beaten-track villages such as Pernand-Vergelesses or St Aubin, where good well-priced wines can be tasted and bought. Most villages in Burgundy have a *caveau*, or wine shop. The choice may not always be scintillating, but there are exceptions, such as an excellent wine shop in the center of Chassagne-Montrachet.

The best way to visit Burgundy is to take your time over it. Three days is about right. Base yourself in Beaune for convenience, visit the BIVB (*see* page 29) to acquire maps and winery lists, make a handful of appointments and book your evening meals in advance.

Some classic culinary specialties to try include coq au vin, boeuf bourguignon, the terrine-like *jambon persillé*, snails, and the rich poached-egg dish *oeufs en meurette*. These are widely available, but the best Burgundian cooking is less traditional in approach. On the other hand, every good restaurant serves the wonderful regional cheeses.

There are restaurants to suit every pocket, and there is no need to spend a fortune to eat and drink well. Two simple restaurants with large, but inexpensive, wine lists are Ma Cuisine in Beaune and Aux Vendanges de Bourgogne in Gevrey-Chambertin.

The best time to visit Burgundy is in the spring and fall. It is very crowded in early summer, and in August everyone is on holiday, resting before the harvest. Nor is it sensible to visit during the hectic harvest period, when producers are busy. Also avoid late November, when the celebrated charity auction at the Hospices takes place.

BURGUNDY

MAIN GRAPES

Red: Pinot noir.

White: Chardonnay.

LEADING WINE VILLAGES AND PRODUCERS

(Producers named are those that are open to the public.
Grand Cru vineyards are in brackets.)

CÔTE DE NUITS:

Gevrey-Chambertin: Philippe Leclerc (Chambertin,
Mazy-Chambertin).

Morey-St-Denis: (Clos de la Roche).

Chambolle-Musigny: (Bonnes Mares, Musigny).

Vougeot: Bertagna (Clos Vougeot).

Vosne-Romanée: Bruno Clavelier (Richebourg, Echezeaux).

Nuits-St-Georges: Daniel Rion.

CÔTE DE BEAUNE:

Savigny-les-Beaune

Aloxe-Corton: (Corton-Charlemagne for white, Corton
for red).

Beaune: Joseph Drouhin, Patriarche.

Pommard

Volnay

Meursault: Château de Meursault.

Puligny-Montrachet: Chartron et Trebuchet (Montrachet,
Bâtard-Montrachet, Chevalier-Montrachet).

Chassagne-Montrachet: (Montrachet, Bâtard-Montrachet).

CÔTE CHALONNAISE:

Mercurey: Antonin Rodet, Michel Juillot.

Rully

Givry

Montagny.

ABOVE LEFT The Confrèrie du Tastevin's band entertains guests with
traditional songs at a banquet at Clos de Vougeot.

ABOVE RIGHT Harvest time at Aloxe-Corton. A picker tips a *hotte*
(pannier) of pinot noir grapes into a waiting tractor.

MAIN TOWNS Dijon, Beaune.

AIRPORTS Paris, Lyons.

DAYS One to seven.

BEST TIME TO GO March to June;
mid-October to mid-November.

SUMMARY Dijon – Nuits-St-
Georges – Beaune – Chagny –
Chalon-sur-Saône.

SOURCES OF
INFORMATION

• *Bureau Interprofessionnel*
des Vins de Bourgogne (BIVB)
12 Boulevard Bretonnière,
21204 Beaune, France.
Tel: +33 80.25.04.80
Fax: +33 80.25.04.90.
Email: bivb@wanadoo.fr

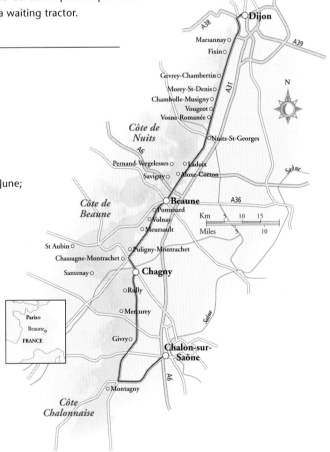

THE LOIRE

ANJOU-SAUMUR AND TOURAINE

JIM BUDD

The Loire has a special sense of light and space, large quantities of honey-colored building stone, a mix of large and small rivers and a proximity to Paris. It is small wonder that the French kings and their court were utterly seduced by the gentle landscape and climate of the Loire Valley and spent much of the Renaissance years there.

The Loire is 620 miles (1000 kilometers) long, rising only about 90 miles (150 kilometers) from the Mediterranean before heading north and then west to the Atlantic Ocean. The Loire and its tributaries drain two-fifths of France. The heart and best-known part of the valley is the Val de Loire from Blois westwards to Angers. This is much of the area that has been declared a World Heritage Site by UNESCO. All the region's famous châteaux are located here: the grandiose Chambord, the perfection of Chenonceau across the River Cher, the exquisite Azay-le-Rideau on the Indre, the sombre fortress of Saumur that dominates the town after which it is named, and many others. As well as these world-renowned icons, there are hundreds of other lesser known châteaux and manor houses hidden in the landscape.

The Loire is an important climate boundary. It divides the cooler, wetter north of France from the warmer, drier south. The climate is temperate, and there are rarely extremes of temperature, as the Atlantic has a moderating influence. This is also one of France's two most northerly wine regions. The other is Champagne, to the east of Paris, which makes largely sparkling wine, because of the difficulty ripening the grapes fully in that chilly climate.

Unlike many other French regions the Loire does not really have its own distinctive cuisine. There are a few local specialties such as *rillettes*, a potted meat made from pork or goose;

LEFT The imposing 14th-century Château de Saumur dominates both the Loire and the attractive old town of Saumur, which makes a good base for exploring Anjou-Saumur and the vineyards of Chinon and Bourgueil.

andouillettes, tripe sausages from Vouvray; and *fuyé,* which has some similarity to pitta bread and is filled with *rillettes* or beans. The region is famous for goat's cheese, which goes rather better with white wine than with red. Otherwise the cooking is classic French since this was the home of the court. Intriguingly, the birth of French fine cooking is often ascribed to Catherine de Medici, who brought along her Italian chefs when she married the Duke of Orléans, the future Henry II, in 1533.

Friendly family producers are the norm in the Loire. Throughout the region you will find signs inviting you to visit, taste, and buy. Just make sure that you do not turn up between midday and 2:00 and disturb the producers' sacred lunch break!

Our tour starts in Angers with its imposing cathedral and forbidding château. North of the Loire, Angers is a lively town with many hotels and restaurants. From here it is only a short excursion to the small town of Brissac in the Coteaux de l'Aubance (*coteaux* means steep slopes) with its very tall Renaissance château. As well as making sweet wines, Brissac is the center of red wine in Anjou. At the Domaine de Bablut, the Daviau family has been making wine since 1546.

To the west of Angers, the vineyards of Savennières and, in particular, the famous Coulée de Serrant, are among the few vineyards in Anjou on the north bank of the Loire. It is here that chenin blanc, the great and versatile white grape of the Loire, is first

known to have been planted. Chenin has the remarkable capacity to make fine dry wines, luscious sweet wines and well-balanced demi-secs (medium-sweet wines). There is a distinct sense of old wealth in Savennières, which has a number of imposing 18th- and 19th-century properties built by prosperous merchants who moved out of Angers to seek space and quiet.

Rochefort, a small town on the opposite bank of the Loire, is close to the Coteaux du Layon, Anjou's famous sweet wine-producing region. The road going east out of Rochefort takes you up to Chaume and the Quarts de Chaume, one of the best sites in France for sweet wine. Here the steep-sided Layon Valley is ideal for encouraging botrytis (noble rot) in the fall, when cool misty mornings give way to warm, sunny days. The vines are picked several times and the harvest can last until late November. The best way to see the vineyards is to criss-cross the valley via small roads, visiting villages such as St Aubin, St Lambert-du-Lattay, and Faye d'Anjou.

Moving a little further east Thouarcé has the famous sweet wine appellation of Bonnezeaux. The best-known property here is Château de Fesles, which is on top of the ridge with its vineyards facing south over the valley. Thouarcé marks the end of the most interesting part of the Layon.

Travel eastwards past Doué la Fontaine to the attractive little town of Montreuil-Bellay and its enchanting château by the banks of the River Thouet, which joins the Loire close to Saumur. Avoid the main highway and take a minor road through the vineyards by the village of Coudray-Macouard to Saumur.

The historic but lively town of Saumur makes a good base to explore the vineyards, both here and in Chinon and Bourgeuil. This is the center of sparkling wine production in the Loire, making around 15 million bottles annually. The *tuffeau* (soft limestone) makes it easy to excavate cellars, whose darkness and constant temperature are ideal for aging the wine during its secondary fermentation.

Two of the leading houses are Bouvet-Laduby, which has an art museum, and Gratien et Meyer. Many cellars started as quarries, with the *tuffeau* being cut out to construct the châteaux and other buildings.

Around Saumur are the vineyards of Saumur-Champigny, which produce one of the best red wines of the Loire, made from cabernet franc. Although in Bordeaux and other parts of the world cabernet franc is less famous than cabernet sauvignon, it does well here as it ripens early and so is suited to the Loire's cooler climate. Explore the network of small roads to the east of Saumur, going through villages such as Chacé, Champigny and Parnay. There are also some fine dry whites made in this area from chenin blanc.

Before entering Touraine, you should make time for a little sightseeing. Alongside the Loire, the towns of Montsoreau with its château, and Candes St Martin with its narrow streets, are worth a quick visit. Candes St Martin, which is situated at the

confluence of the Vienne and the Loire rivers, forms the boundary between Saumur and Touraine. About 3 miles (5 kilometers) south of Montsoreau is the Abbaye of Fontrevaud which merits a visit. Magnificently restored, it is the burial place of the Plantagenets, a line of English kings who ruled much of western France and England in the Middle Ages.

The three best red wine villages of Touraine – Bourgueil, St Nicolas de Bourgueil and Chinon – are close together. Again the main grape variety is cabernet franc. Chinon is the best known because Rabelais, the 16th-century cleric and physician, and the author of *Gargantua* and *Pantagruel*, was born nearby. Here, wines from good vintages can age a surprising length of time, especially those from the Clos d'Echo, the most famous vineyard of Chinon, whose 1964 vintage is still very drinkable although hard to find.

Bourgueil has a fine Benedictine abbey that dates from 990, but Chinon, with its ancient streets and houses, is the prettiest town to visit. The best views are from the south bank of the Vienne, with the ruined château dominating the small medieval town huddling below. Chinon's leading producer, Couly-Dutheil, has cellars in the town. Some dry white from chenin blanc is also made.

Apart from a few vines around Azay-le-Rideau, there are no significant vineyards between Chinon and those of Vouvray and Montlouis, east of Tours. They can be reached by going through the busy city of Tours, with its medieval and 19th-century quarters. Alternatively take the back roads along the valley of the Indre and then cut up towards Montlouis. The wines of Montlouis and Vouvray are made from chenin blanc. Styles range from austerely dry to concentrated sweetness. Everything depends upon the weather; in some years, like 1947 and 1959, it is possible to make amazing, concentrated wines that can age almost for ever. In less favorable years only dry and sparkling wines

are possible. It is worth exploring the network of little roads that lead up into the vineyards. Huet SA is the most famous producer in Vouvray and has long been a byword for quality.

The vineyards to the east of Vouvray and Montlouis are only entitled to the general Touraine appellation but they often offer good value. Continue onwards from Vouvray or Montlouis via Amboise, a busy and charming town, to the smaller but also pretty Montrichard in the Cher Valley. Many of the best vineyards are found on either side of the Cher Valley, to the east of Montrichard, especially around the villages of Pouillé, Oisly and Thesée. One of the best Loire co-operatives is in Oisly.

ABOVE With its gables, turrets and tranquil reflective moat, the Château d' Azay-le-Rideau is one of the jewels of the Loire.
BELOW The Clos de l'Echo at Chinon is one of the region's top red vineyards. Now owned by Couly-Dutheil, it was once the property of the family of 16th-century French writer François Rabelais.

MAIN GRAPES

White: Chenin blanc, sauvignon blanc.
Red: Cabernet franc, gamay.

LEADING WINES (APPELLATIONS)

Anjou-Saumur, Anjou Blanc, Anjou Rouge, Anjou
Villages, Bonnezeaux, Coteaux de l'Aubance,
Coteaux du Layon, Quarts de Chaume, Saumur,
Saumur Champigny, Anjou-Saumur-Touraine, Crémant
de Loire, Touraine, Bourgueil, Cheverney, Chinon,
St Nicolas de Bourgueil, Montlouis, Touraine, Vouvray.

MAIN PRODUCERS

ANJOU-SAUMUR *(Most producers in Anjou make a wide
range of wines.)*
Coteaux de l'Aubance: Bablut.
Savennières and **Coteaux du Layon:** Baumard,
Ogereau.
Saumur: Bouvet-Ladubay, Caves de Vignerons de St
Cyr, Gratien et Meyer (sparkling Saumur).
Saumur-Champigny: Domaine de Nerleux, Filliatreau,
Ch de Villeneuve.
Bonnezeaux: Ch de Fesles.
TOURAINE
Chinon: Bernard Baudry, Couly-Dutheil.
Touraine: Christophe and Jean Baudry, Confrèrie des
Vignerons de Oisly et Thésée, Marionnet.
Vouvray: Foreau, Huet SA.
Montlouis: Taille aux Loups.

MAIN TOWNS Angers, Saumur, Tours.

AIRPORTS Paris (Charles de Gaulle and Orly),
Nantes.

DAYS One week.

BEST TIME TO GO April to October.

SUMMARY Angers – Layon Valley – Doué la
Fontaine – Montreuil-Bellay – Saumur – Chinon – Azay-
le-Rideau – Tours – Vouvray – Amboise – Montrichard.

SOURCES OF INFORMATION
• *Maison du Vin de l'Anjou*
5 bis Place Kennedy, 49100 Angers.
Tel: +33 02.41.88.81.13.

FAR LEFT A typical troglodyte house cut into the
tufa (limestone) at Vouvray.
LEFT The grandiose Château de Chambord,
François I's modest hunting lodge!

• *Maison des Vins de Saumur*
Quai Lucien Gauthier, 49400, Saumur.
Tel: +33 02.41.51.16.40.
• *Comité Interprofessionnel des Vins d'Appellation
d'Origine de la Touraine et du Coeur Val de Loire (CIVTL)*
19 square Prosper Mérimée, 3700 Tours.
Tel: +33 02.47.05.40.01.
Web: www.interloire.com

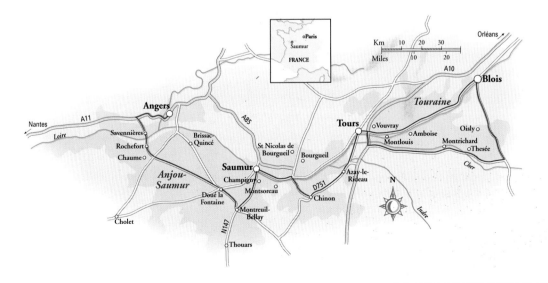

THE RHÔNE

JOHN LIVINGSTONE-LEARMONTH

The northern Rhône valley marks the start of the south of France. Heading towards the Mediterranean, the landscape loses its northern lush green intensity; the pasture becomes plainer and grazing animals are replaced by fruit trees and vines. The evenings stay warm, and dining outdoors is the custom in summer. The red wines are rich, fed by ripe grapes. This is the home of the syrah, an ancient variety known as shiraz in other parts of the world.

Much of the area is underlaid by the granite of central France, the Massif Central, away to the west. This brings out the complex, dark berry, sometimes peppery, fruit found in the syrah wines of the major vineyards at Côte-Rôtie, Hermitage, and Cornas.

The northern Rhône is a small region. The vineyards which flank the river are largely composed of masses of hillside ledges, narrow and often precarious. The views are tight, taking the eye skywards rather than towards a horizon. The cellars are small and simple. A typical holding at Côte-Rotie or Cornas is rarely more than 12 acres (5 hectares). If you intend visiting a cellar, phone the grower beforehand: there are few formal reception areas, and visitors usually meet the family, not an intermediary.

The winemaking tradition here precedes the Romans, going back to 500BC via the Phocacean Greeks, founders of Marseille. These seafarers saw the virtue of the Rhône as a channel for trade. It remains the link between the Mediterranean and Switzerland, and is the natural conduit for tourism heading south.

Travelers today have a choice of the autoroutes, which get clogged up at peak weekends in summer, or taking the more leisurely western route south, using the N86 that runs past the mountain streams and caves of the Ardèche, where the villages are washed in pale brown colors, many of the churches are Romanesque, and apricots, cherries, and wines from the area

LEFT La Chapelle, on the main granite site of the Hill of Hermitage, overlooks Tain l'Hermitage and Tournon which straddle the Rhône below. The vineyard in the foreground is owned by the family firm of Chapoutier.

are for sale beside the road. Another exciting option is the high speed TGV train, which makes the 650-mile (1045-kilometer) journey from Calais to Marseille in about three hours.

The Côte-Rôtie appellation is centered on the nondescript village of Ampuis, home of Marcel Guigal's large wine empire. Its prime sites are beside and above the village, on the Côte Brune and Côte Blonde. Impressive from the road, the full scale of the slope and the hard work involved becomes clear if you drive up the winding trails to the top plateau.

At many points south until Cornas, take the opportunity to head off the N86 and up the side roads in among the vineyards. Côte-

Rôtie is the most delicate of Rhône reds. The bouquet is often floral and, in a stunning year (such as 1999), it is ample, juicy and generous. It is a wonderful wine, a true bridge between Burgundy and the Rhône.

The whole northern Rhône has thrived in the past 20 years, but the most amazing comeback has been at Condrieu, a vineyard on the point of disappearance in the late 1960s, when just 25 acres (10 hectares) were cultivated. Now there are over 250 acres (100 hectares) under vines. Condrieu's signature grape, viognier, ranks alongside varietals such as muscat with its embracing muskiness, a scent mixing blossoms and fresh pears, and a flavor that provides apricot, pear, and honey tones. Very full, it is delightful with local dishes like *quenelles au brochet* (moussed pike) or *turbot au champagne*, which are served in the best restaurants, like the Beau Rivage at Condrieu, where the terrace beside the Rhône provides a great summer idyll. Beau Rivage also provides comfortable rooms.

Dotted along the west bank south of Condrieu are some of the Saint-Joseph villages: Chavanay with its fine church, the pretty and isolated Malleval, Serrières with its water-jousting tradition and top hotel-restaurant Schaeffer, and Sarras, which has great Ardèche views. These villages produce fruity, quite full white wines (from marsanne with some roussanne grapes) and exuberant black-fruit-flavored reds, from pure syrah.

Saint-Joseph and Crozes-Hermitage reds are good restaurant choices, their abundant early fruit complementing meat and *charcuterie* dishes. Hermitage and Cornas are natural selections with game and richer main courses, while Côte-Rôtie is excellent with lamb.

The center of the northern Rhône is the appellation of Hermitage, on the river's east bank. The most enduring Rhône wines, both red and white, come from the hill which rises behind the modest town of Tain l'Hermitage, whose hilltop chapel is illuminated at night. Cross the footbridge which spans the river

between the towns of Tain and Tournon for a view of both hillside vineyards and to capture a sense of the Rhône's sturdy power.

Tain houses the *négociant* Chapoutier, and a good, if expensive, wine store on the main Place Taurobole. The hotels are clean and modest, in line with the region's general profile. In Tournon, the restaurant Chaudron has the best wine list in the northern Rhône, at very fair prices. Tournon is where the steam train to Lamastre leaves on its summer runs.

Beyond Tournon the road never runs far from the Rhône, passing Mauves, a prime site for Saint-Joseph, and the striking château of Châteaubourg, leading to Cornas, home of the mighty dark red wine that opens and mellows after eight-plus years. The tiny cellars of the main growers such as Auguste Clape, Thiérry Allemand and Noël Verset typify the region's viticultural past.

The last Northern Rhône appellation, Saint-Péray, produces both still and sparkling white wines from marsanne and roussanne.

Notable growers include Gripa, Chaboud and Lionnet. Near the busy city of Valence, the area is mainstream in feel, unlike old-style Cornas, but the roads to St Romain-de-Lerps or Lamastre plunge the visitor back into conventional rural views and traditions.

Leaving the vineyards of the northern Rhône behind you, continue traveling south and, after a vine-free interval of 40 miles (64 kilometers), the southern Rhône spreads out beyond Donzère. Here, the panoramas open up, and the senses are tempted by the soft aromas of lavender and herbs on the air and by the growing radiance of the sun, with its penetrating light. No wonder artists like van Gogh and Picasso came here to paint.

The plains and hills sloping east towards the Alps are fully planted with vines, the region's main crop, interspersed with olives and some fruit trees. From west of Valréas come black truffles. Beaugravière restaurant at Mondragon offers an array of truffle-based dishes backed by a fabulous wine list.

The southern Rhône is built around the grenache grape, marking a shift of style from the black fruit flavors of the syrah. The reds here are more heated, more potent, and convey plum and cooked fruit flavors with herbal tones. In the Côtes-du-Rhône Villages category, try dark robust Rasteau or the red-fruited Cairanne, Séguret and Sablet. Ventoux and Lubéron are other fringe areas of note.

Many villages cluster around concentric streets that loop and run below their church. Tiny main squares allow *pétanque* (boules or bowls) playing and serve as a social forum. Given the fecundity of the land, markets are a colorful part of life in the southern Rhône. The most important ones are in the big towns like Orange (not easy to find parking) and Avignon, but try to go to Uzès, in the Gard, on a Saturday, or to Carpentras. The smaller villages also have weekly markets for fresh food and vegetables, with a good selection of cheeses (often goat), herbs, honey, nuts, lavender, garlic, and wild mushrooms.

The wine capital of the southern Rhône is Châteauneuf-du-Pape, world-famous for its big-tasting, ripe red wines. With over 7900 acres (3200 hectares), it is the Rhône's largest appellation. By comparison, tiny Hermitage is just 309 acres (125 hectares). The area is covered with pale rust-colored stones, called *galets*, left by the shifting of old Alpine glaciers; they hide a generally-clay subsoil with some sandy patches nearer the rivers.

Wine tasting is well-organized in both the village of Châteauneuf-du-Pape and the domaines throughout the vineyard, which runs east to Courthézon and Bédarrides. Dropping in without an appointment is more fruitful here than in the northern Rhône. Châteauneuf-du-Pape's good vintages from 1998 to 2001 are excellent buys.

From the plateau just north of Châteauneuf-du-Pape there is a stunning view across to the Dentelles de Montmirail, a series of spiky rocks beside the village of Gigondas, and to Mont Ventoux, which can be snow-topped. The vineyards here are often cleansed by the powerful north wind, the Mistral, which opens up the skies and blows ferociously for days at a time.

Gigondas is home to a tasty, ripe, full red wine with less softness than Châteauneuf-du-Pape, which is best drunk with strong food, notably meat and game dishes. It is flanked by a finer, more delicate red wine from Vacqueyras. With less overt tannins than those of Gigondas and a very typical grenache pepperiness, it is good value for money.

The next-door village of Beaumes-de-Venise produces the Rhône's sweet wine, the honey/grapey-scented Muscat. Explore the road to Lafare and Suzette and try to spot the wild boar and deer that roam in the woods.

The many villages between the Vaucluse and the Drôme, further north around Vinsobres, are an area of star value. The wines here have made great progress in the last decade. In the Drôme they have a cooler red fruit texture and finer tannins, while in the Vaucluse they are riper and more forceful. Here, the grenache is always mixed with other varietals, such as syrah, mourvèdre and cinsaut, to make a spicy cocktail. Domaines are well signposted and the driving is easy. Good hotels include the tucked-away Les Florêts near Gigondas and the welcoming La Mère Germaine in Châteauneuf-du-Pape. Dishes served in local restaurants such as Mas de Bouvau and Castel Mireio near Cairanne often include lamb, sea bass, or mullet.

Across the Rhône from Avignon lies the Gard, once a center for Huguenot beliefs and still marching to a simpler tempo than the Vaucluse. The red wines are softer, while good rosé and white wines come from villages like Lirac, Laudun, and St Victor-la-Coste. There is a sense of escapism when traveling the often-forested roads between the Roman village of Pont-du-Gard and Bagnols-sur-Cèze. Domaines here are less equipped for visitors, except in the main center of Tavel, home of a full-tasting rosé.

THE RHÔNE

MAIN GRAPES

NORTHERN RHÔNE

Red: Syrah.

White: Marsanne, roussanne, viognier.

SOUTHERN RHÔNE

Red: Grenache, syrah, mourvèdre.

White: Clairette, grenache blanc, bourboulenc, roussanne.

LEADING WINES (APPELLATIONS)

N. Rhône: Côte-Rôtie, Hermitage, Cornas, Saint-Joseph, St-Peray, Crozes-Hermitage, Condrieu.

S. Rhône: Châteauneuf-du-Pape, Gigondas, Vacqueyras, Lirac, Tavel, Beaumes-de-Venise, Côtes-du-Rhône Villages.

MAIN PRODUCERS

Côte-Rôtie: Barge, Burgaud, Clusel-Roch, Guigal, G. Bernard, Gérin, Jamet, Jasmin, Ogier.

Hermitage: Chapoutier, Chave, Delas, Faurie, Paul Jaboulet Aîné, Sorrel.

Cornas: Allemand, Clape, Verset, Voge.

Crozes-Hermitage: Belle, Y Chave, Combier, Desmeure, Graillot, Pochon, Viale.

Saint-Joseph: Coursodon, Gonon, Gripa, Perret.

Condrieu: Perret, Vernay, Verzier.

Châteauneuf-du-Pape: Château Beaucastel, Nerthe, Rayas, Clos du Mont Olivet, des Papes, Domaines Beaurenard, Bosquet des Papes, Cailloux, Font-de-Michelle, Vieille Julienne, Vieux Télégraphe, Villeneuve.

Gigondas: Domaines Cayron, Font-Sane, Les Goubert, Grapillon d'Or, Raspail-Ay, St-Gayan, Santa Duc, Pallières.

Vacqueyras: Domaines Couroulu, Fourmone, Garrigue, Monardière, Sang des Cailloux.

Lirac: Aquéria, Château d'Aquéria, Domaines Fermade, Mordorée, Sabon.

Tavel: Aquéria, Corne-Loup, Montezargues, Mordorée, Trinquevedel.

Beaumes-de-Venise: Domaines Coyeux, Durban, Fenouillet.

Côtes-du-Rhône/CdR Villages: Fonsalette, Château Courançonne, Hugues, Redortier, Domaines Alary, Romain Bouchard, Brusset, Cros de la Mûre, Gramenon, Grand Moulas, Oratoire St Martin, Pelaquié, Piaugier, Réméjeanne, Richaud, Ste-Anne, Soumade, Vieux-Chêne.

MAIN TOWNS/ AIRPORTS

Lyon, Marseille, Avignon, Valence.

DAYS

Northern Rhône: two days. Southern Rhône: three days.

BEST TIME TO GO

April to October.

ABOVE Top Côte-Rôtie producers such as Marcel Guigal give their best syrah wines 42 months in new oak barrels, making them extremely expensive, and rare.

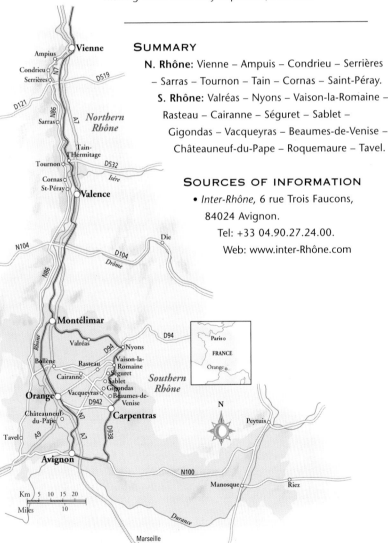

SUMMARY

N. Rhône: Vienne – Ampuis – Condrieu – Serrières – Sarras – Tournon – Tain – Cornas – Saint-Péray.

S. Rhône: Valréas – Nyons – Vaison-la-Romaine – Rasteau – Cairanne – Séguret – Sablet – Gigondas – Vacqueyras – Beaumes-de-Venise – Châteauneuf-du-Pape – Roquemaure – Tavel.

SOURCES OF INFORMATION

• *Inter-Rhône*, 6 rue Trois Faucons, 84024 Avignon.
  Tel: +33 04.90.27.24.00.
  Web: www.inter-Rhône.com

LANGUEDOC

ROSEMARY GEORGE MW

Landing at Montpellier, a city near France's Mediterranean coast, is dramatic. The plane turns out at sea, descending over the *étangs*, the saltwater lakes, with their oyster beds and pink flamingos. You might even see a patch of vines from the runway, for these are the coastal plains where vines grow effortlessly and prolifically. In the distance are the hazy silhouettes of the foothills of the Massif Central, the peaks that dominate the skyline of the Languedoc vineyards.

Leave the bustle of Montpellier behind you, and head towards the town of St Martin-de-Londres, with its gem of a Romanesque church, to the vineyards of Pic St Loup. The eponymous mountain, which dominates the skyline, also gives its name to the wine, one of the most elegant of the various crus (smaller and better areas) of the Coteaux du Languedoc, produced in a cluster of villages around the peak and the similarly stark Montagne de l'Hortus.

Pic St Loup is characteristic of the startling changes that have overtaken the Languedoc in the last 10 years or so. Quite simply, the Languedoc used to be known as a producer of cheap, but not necessarily cheerful, *vin ordinaire* or *vin de table* (everyday wine). Growing grapes on the coastal plain was easy and viticulture was undemanding, but the flavors were dilute and insipid. Producers were paid by hectolitre and alcoholic degree, with flavor a very secondary consideration. But over the last few years, the value of the hilly vineyard sites to the north of Montpellier has been rediscovered and there has been a general shift towards quality viticulture away from the coast. Working conditions in the hills are much tougher, for the vineyards themselves are dry and stony. The scenery is wild and rugged, dominated by the dramatic peak. The wines speak very much of the place; they have warmth and backbone and convey the scents of the herbs of the *garrigue*, the scrubland which covers hillsides all over the Midi, as the south of France is known.

LEFT Hand picking is still practised by smaller producers, such as Château Lahore-Bergez in the Aude – who need whole bunches for carbonic maceration – although mechanical harvesting has taken over in larger vineyards.

Ten years ago the local cooperative was the one producer of any significance in this region; in contrast today there is a growing number of independent producers working to establish a reputation for themselves and their region. They have abandoned the inferior grape varieties to concentrate on the so-called *cépages améliorateurs*, or improving grape varieties, such as syrah and, to a lesser extent, mourvèdre.

Traveling west, the next significant area of the Coteaux du Languedoc is Montpeyroux, where the vineyards surround the small village. Once again production was formerly dominated by the village cooperative, which has now been joined by several independent producers who are questioning many of the accepted practices of the region. Not only has there been a shift to better vineyard sites, but cellar practices have improved with the introduction of temperature control and the replacement of larger oak vats by small wooden barrels, all in the quest for quality and character. This makes Languedoc an exciting and challenging place to visit. In contrast to some parts of France, where long-established practices remain unquestioned, any producer in the Midi worth their salt is constantly seeking to do better.

Between Pic St Loup and Montpeyroux are the dramatic Gorges de l'Hérault, with the enchanting abbey of St Guilhem-le-Désert and the Roman bridge of Pont du Diable.

ABOVE LEFT André Leenhardt in his barrel cellar at Château de Cazeneuve, a leading Pic St Loup estate. Like many winemakers, this is a second career for him.
LEFT Domaine l'Hortus nestles beneath mountains of the same name near St Mathieu-de-Tréviers, Hérault. Jean Orliac first saw his future vineyards while rock climbing there as a student.
OPPOSITE Mas de Daumas Gassac in Aniane. In the distant Gorges de l'Hérault, the organically-farmed vineyards have been cut out of patches of *garrigue*.

At nearby Aniane is Mas de Daumas Gassac, a visitor-friendly estate which has done much to establish the reputation of the Languedoc, in this case, not for appellation wines but for humble *vin de pays*, planting cabernet sauvignon to make what owner, Aimé Guibert, would like to call a first growth of the Languedoc. The village of St Saturnin hosts a *fête du vin nouveau* on the middle Sunday in October. In the adjacent village of St Guiraud, Le Mimosa has one of the best tables of the region and a wine list to match.

Both Faugères and St Chinian became appellations in their own right in 1982, before being incorporated into the all-embracing Coteaux du Languedoc. The tiny village of Faugères has nothing to delay the visitor apart from its wine estates; Roquessels with its ruined castle has more charm, while the town of St Chinian is more substantial. There is a Maison du Vin at one end of the plane-tree-lined square, which offers tastings of St Chinian to passing visitors, and a tempting wine shop, Espace Vin, nearby with a good selection of local wines.

The village of Roquebrun, at the southern end of the Gorges de l'Orb, is a peaceful place to stay. In the main street, a New Zealand couple run a friendly bed and breakfast, Les Mimosas; and yet another ruined castle testifies to the troubled history of the region. The village cooperative here is working hard to improve the quality of its wine, alongside many independent producers.

The appellation of Minervois adjoins St Chinian, with a tiny enclave of sweet wine made from muscat at St Jean de Minervois. The village of Minerve, perched on steep cliffs, gave its name to the appellation, in turn taking its name from the Roman goddess of wisdom, Minerva. In the Albigensian crusade of the late 12th century, the siege of Minerve ended with numerous members of the Cathar sect leaping to their deaths from the cliffs.

The wines here are very much like the countryside, wild and sturdy, with warm powerful flavors. Although there is white Minervois, red wine is much more important.

The highest vineyards are on the foothills of the Montagne Noire but as you go south, the countryside becomes gentle and undulating, until you reach the valley of the Aude and the Canal du Midi, with numerous sleepy villages where little happens apart from wine making. Olonzac comes to life on market day, and La Livinière is establishing itself as a cru within the appellation.

Across the Aude valley the skyline is dominated by the Montagne d'Alaric, the highest mountain of the northern part of the appellation of Corbières, while to the south there is Mont Tauch. On a clear day you can see the snow-capped mountains of the Pyrenees with the Pic du Canigou. This is another area of little villages, and the wild scenery of rocky hillsides is often topped by ruined Cathar castles, such as Quéribus, Durban and, the finest of all, Peyrepertuse. The little town of Lagrasse, with its abbey and Roman bridge, is an attractive place to stop,

while the nearby abbey of Fontfroide is altogether more splendid and imposing.

Corbières is one of the larger appellations of France. Again red is the principal color, with a shift away from carignan to syrah and mourvèdre, with grenache noir.

The art of blending is an essential part of all the appellation wines of the Languedoc, which do not depend on one single variety alone, as many other *vins de pays* do.

Mixed with Corbières are the vineyards of Fitou, the earliest appellation for table wine, as opposed to fortified wine, in the Languedoc. This is a split appellation, with vineyards around Tuchan and Mont Tauch, as well as vineyards on the coast around the village of Fitou itself.

Now it is time to turn east again. The highway, la Languedocienne, provides a fast artery, permitting various detours, such as to the Roman city of Narbonne, with its unfinished cathedral, St Just. Outside Beziers,

at Fonsérunes, there is a flight of eight locks, an extraordinary engineering achievement of the 17th century, which enabled the Canal du Midi to link the Mediterranean to the Atlantic. Pézenas is a welcoming town, with its old quarters and narrow streets. The nearby Abbaye de Valmagne is known not only for its wine, but also for its breathtakingly beautiful cloisters and chapter house. The Massif de la Clape, outside Narbonne, is part of the Coteaux du Languedoc, while further east there are the vineyards of Picpoul de Pinet, an island of white wine in a sea of red. Enjoy a glass of Picpoul with oysters, looking over the oyster beds at Bouzigues on the coast, and all will seem very right with the world.

TOP The attractive village of Roquebrun, in the cru of St Chinian, perched on cliffs above the river Orb, is dominated by the ruins of a medieval castle.

LANGUEDOC

LEFT The landscape of Languedoc simply bursts with promise. Here, rocky foothills tower over a verdant valley where vines ripen to perfection in the warm Mediterranean sun.

MAIN GRAPES

Red: Syrah, mourvèdre, grenache noir, carignan and cinsaut for appellation wines. Cabernet sauvignon, merlot and pinot noir are allowed for *vins de pays*.
White: Grenache blanc, bourboulenc, macabeu, ugni blanc, clairette, marsanne, roussanne, rolle (vermentino); muscat á petits grains and muscat d'Alexandrie for *vin doux naturel*; chardonnay, sauvignon, viognier and terret blanc for *vins de pays*.

LEADING WINES (APPELLATIONS) AND PRODUCERS

Fitou: Co-opérative des Producteurs de Mont Tauch, Domaine Rolland.
Corbières: Domaine la Voulte-Gasparets, Domaine Serres-Mazard, Château du Vieux-Parc, Château Lastours, Domaine St Auriol, Domaine du Trillol.
Minervois: Château de Gourgazaud, Domaine Villerambert-Julien, Château Coupe-Roses, Château la Grave, Domaine la Combe Blanche, Domaine Borie de Maurel, Clos Centeilles.
Coteaux du Languedoc: (*Most important subregions in* **bold italics***, others in italics.*)
la Clape: Château Pech-Redon, Château Rouquette-sur-Mer.
Picpoul de Pinet: Domaine Félines-Jourdan.
St Chinian: Domaine des Jougla, Borie la Vitarèle, Mas Champart, Domaine Canet-Valette, Domaine Moulinier.
Faugères: Domaine Alquier, Domaine des Estanilles, Domaine du Météore.

Pic St Loup: Domaine l'Hortus, Château Lavabre, Mas Bruguière, Château Cazeneuve.
Montpeyroux: Domaine Aupilhac, Domaine de Font Caude.
*Others***:** Prieuré de St Jean de Bébian, Château de Flaugergues, Abbaye de Valmagne.
Muscat de St Jean de Minervois: Domaine Barroubio.
Vin de Pays d'Oc: Domaine de la Baume, Fortant de France, James Herrick, Domaine Virginie, Domaine la Chevalière.
Vin de Pays des Côtes de Thongue: Domaine la Croix-Belle, Domaine de l'Arjolle, Prieuré d'Amilhac, Domaine de la Condamine l'Evêque.
Vin de Pays de l'Hérault: Mas de Daumas Gassac, Domaine la Grange des Pères.

AIRPORTS Montpellier, Carcassonne.

DAYS One to two weeks. You could have a wonderful fortnight's touring holiday enjoying the history and scenery as well as the wine, or simply dip into the region for a long weekend.

BEST TIME TO GO April to June; September and October. Avoid the heat of summer.

SUMMARY Montpellier – Pic St Loup – Montpeyroux – Faugères – St Chinian – St Jean de Minervois – Lézignan-Corbières – Fitou – la Clape – Picpoul de Pinet.

SOURCES OF INFORMATION

• *Conseil Interprofessionnel des Vins du Languedoc (CIVL)* 9, Cours Mirabeau, 11100 Narbonne
Tel: +33 04.68.90.38.30, Fax: +33 04.68.32.38.00
• *Mas de Saporta*, 34970 Lattes
Tel: +33 04.67.20.88.63
• *Web: www.languedoc-wines.com*

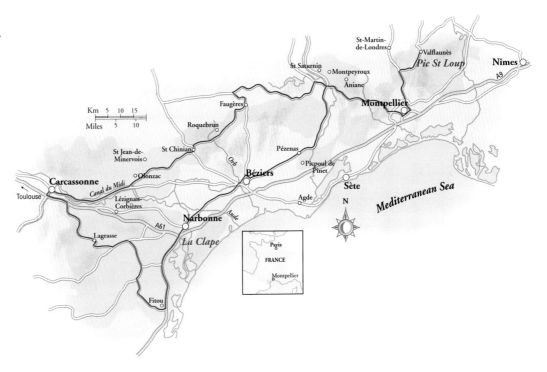

ALSACE

LINDA JOHNSON-BELL

Idyllic medieval villages nestled cozily in voluptuous, fertile hillsides peppered with majestic church steeples, castle ruins, riotous flower displays and pastel-coloured timbered cottages – we are in Alsace. As if the vines were breathing life into the villages, the air is an intoxicating contradiction of spicy fruitiness and mineral freshness. Alsace, with its magic trilogy of history, culture, and gastronomy set against the vivid backdrop of viticulture, makes a perfect picture.

Alsace is one of France's oldest wine-producing regions. There were over 160 wine-growing districts by the end of the first millennium. During the Middle Ages the wines were reputed to be among the best that Europe had to offer. Alsace has been passed back and forth between Germany and France for much of its existence. Despite this continual upheaval and the constant interruptions and destruction caused by war, the wine trade struggled on, and many of the most reputable names are long-established: Dopff (1574), Trimbach (1626), Hugel (1637).

Today, Alsace's 119 wine-growing towns and villages produce more than 160 million bottles, 25 percent of which are exported. Alsace produces 18 percent of the total French still white wine output. Ninety-two percent of Alsace and Alsace Grand Cru wines are dry, aromatic whites. Alsace's appellations are unique in France because the wines are labeled according to grape variety as opposed to the vineyard. Village names appear on all labels, but the vineyard is not always mentioned unless the wine is a Grand Cru, when it is compulsory.

There are seven major grape varieties in Alsace: pinot noir, gewürztraminer, pinot blanc, sylvaner, tokay pinot gris, riesling, and muscat. The wines are organized by quality levels and either belong to the AOC Alsace appellation or to the AOC Grand Cru appellation. The Crémant d'Alsace appellation is for sparkling wine produced in the same way as champagne and mainly from pinot blanc. Then there are levels of ripeness, ranging from dry to two levels of sweetness:

LEFT A 15th-century church rises above Hunawhir, on the Route des Vins. The village is famous for the fabulous Clos Ste-Hune riesling (from the Grand Cru vineyard Rosacker), said to be the best wine of Alsace.

Vendanges Tardives (VT), or late-picked grapes, and *Sélection de Grains Nobles* (SGN), where the grapes have reached even higher sugar levels. VT wines are made using very ripe grapes harvested later than normal, usually in October. SGN wines are made from individually selected botrytized grapes.

The subtly majestic Vosges mountain range protects the region, creating a unique microclimate. Alsace is one of the driest parts of France and enjoys a semi-continental climate, which means lots of sun, heat, and dryness – perfect for the slow, extended hang-time (ripening period) needed by the grapes.

Alsace's white grape varieties do well here because of the patchwork of granite, limestone, gneiss, schist, and sandstone soils which impart acidity and structure to the wine. The vineyards are planted on slopes rather than in the valleys, providing good drainage and enabling them to grow deep roots. The steep slopes also allow the vines to receive the right amount of sunshine at the right time of the day.

While Alsace may appear traditional, it is one of the most forward-thinking wine regions in Europe. The 105 mile (170-kilometer-long) Route des Vins, at the base of the Vosges and alongside the banks of the River Rhine, is tourist-orientated without being kitsch. The Alsatians are neat, organised, and orderly and almost all the villages have a tourist office. The region itself has several award-winning websites and CD ROMs to guide visitors. The wineries are located in the villages and are accessible by foot (most town centers prohibit cars anyway). They are open to the public and offer tastings.

Events are held throughout the year. The spring months are a flurry of costume balls, carnival parades, jazz and classical music concerts and markets. From April to August, every village has its own wine fair with dancing and the copious consumption of local wines and gastronomic specialties.

Harvest Wine Festivals are held in September, October, and November. Then, from 24 November to 7 January, when the picturesque villages are covered in a light blanket of snow, Alsace is transformed. From Colmar to Strasbourg, more than 50 outdoor markets feature illuminated decorations. Bakeries make *mennele* (little bread men), carolers stroll and sing, and Saint Nicholas distributes goodies. There is nothing more enthralling than strolling along a cobbled lane to the sound of an outdoor classical concert, sipping a mug of mulled wine, dodging snowflakes, and admiring the hand-made traditional toys and tree decorations for sale.

Not to be missed are the many regional specialties that so perfectly match the wines. Fresh and fruity sylvaner is ideal with *salade Vosgienne* (mushrooms, red potatoes, Munster cheese, cumin, smoked lardons, croutons, and poached eggs) or with *flammekueche* (a thin flat bread-dough rectangle filled with lightly fried onions, cream, and smoked bacon). Riesling, the pride of Alsace, with its delicate fruit and subtle bouquet, is a perfect partner for *choucroute* (a dish of boiled meats, sauerkraut, and potatoes) or a savoury *kougelhopf* (a brioche filled with perhaps salmon and pike). The full-bodied aromatic gewürztraminer is ideal with spicy exotic dishes, strong cheeses, or the famous *tarte aux pommes à l'Alsacienne*. The easy-going and fresh pinot blanc goes with most anything, but is best with fish. Tokay pinot gris, which falls somewhere between the steely crispness of a riesling and the sweeter opulence of a gewürztraminer, is a perfect match for *baeckaoffa* (a slow-cooked marinated meat stew with onions, potatoes, and seasonings). Alsace pinot noir is light and fruity, almost a rosé. It is especially good with *presskopf* (a terrine of fresh salmon, lobster, and oysters in a creamy sauce of caviar, parsley, tarragon, and chives). Sparkling Crémant d'Alsace is light, refreshing, and crisp. Like champagne, it can accompany an entire meal, from hors d'oeuvres to dessert.

If you have a week available, then start your tour in Strasbourg and head to

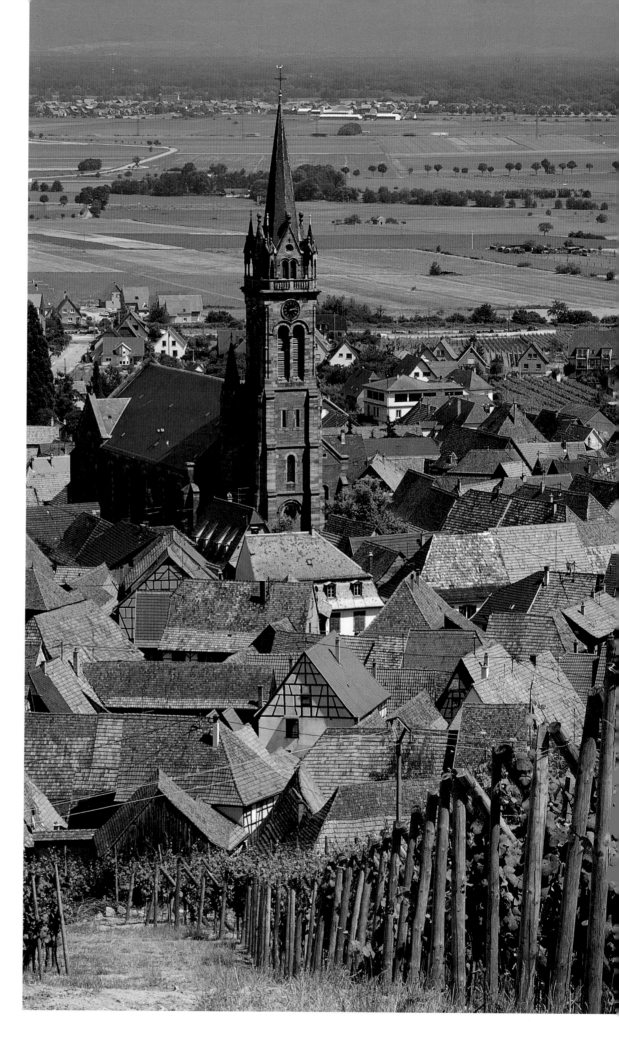

OPPOSITE Ribeauvillé, a thriving tourist center, is famous for its rieslings, wine festivals, restaurants, Christmas market, and the ruins of three castles.

RIGHT The view from the vineyard over the rooftops of Dambach-la-Ville, considered to be the best wine village in the Bas-Rhin.

Marlenheim, the northern gateway to the Route des Vins, and work your way down to Thann, the southernmost point of the route. Both towns have information points that provide maps, guides, and explanations of Alsace's wine history, grapes, and terroirs. If you have only a few days, then make Colmar your base and visit its surrounding villages.

In Colmar, the capital of the Route des Vins, visit the *Bibliothèque* (library) housed in the Dominican Convent; Bartholdi's birthplace (he built New York's Statue of Liberty in 1866); Underlinden Museum, the Maison des Têtes, Maison Pfister, Petit Venise Canal, and Saint-Mattieu's Temple. In August, there is a *foire régionale* (regional fair). For wine tasting, visit Domaine Schoffit.

The village of Bergheim, 12 miles (20 kilometres) north of Colmar, is home to the famous gewürztraminer Grand Cru Altenberg de Bergheim. Taste the wines at Marcel Deiss, Gustave Lorentz or Sylvie Spielmann. Visit the 14th-century Gothic church and upper gateway; walk the vineyard trail; and attend the gewürztraminer feast in August.

Heading towards Colmar, you arrive in Ribeauvillé, with its Grand Cru vineyards of Geisberg, Osterberg and Kirchberg. Taste wine at Henri Fuchs, F.E. Trimbach, Caves de Ribeauvillé, and André Kientzler. Visit the parish church of St Gregory the Great, which was built between the 13th and the 15th centuries, the jewelery museum in the town hall, the remains of the 'three castles' of Ribeaupierre which date from the 12th and 13th centuries, the Renaissance fountain, and the old towers with their stork nests.

ABOVE A traditional bakery in Riquewihr. Very visitor-oriented yet still charming and unspoilt, it is often called the 'Pearl of the Vineyard.'

Just 9 miles (15 kilometers) north of Colmar is Riquewihr, the best preserved medieval and Renaissance village in Alsace and home to the Grands Crus Sporen and Schoenenbourg. Follow the vineyard trail, and take in tastings at Hugel et Fils, Dopff au Moulin, Engel, and Mittnacht Klack. Other attractions include the town's 16th-century fortifications and outer defenses, the 13th-century ruins of Reichenstein castle, and Thieve's Tower Museum, complete with torture chambers.

The next stop on the tour, Kaysersberg, 5 miles (8 kilometers) northwest of Colmar, is famous for its medieval architecture and as the birthplace of Dr. Albert Schweitzer (Nobel Peace Prize 1952). Visit the Renaissance well, castle ruins, fortified bridge and, if you are there at the right time, the famous Christmas market. Taste Domaine Weinbach's riesling, the wines at Cave de Kientzheim-Kayserberg, and Roger Baradel's smoked meats.

One of the best wine villages in Alsace is Ammerschwihr, 5 miles north (8 kilometers) of Colmar. It has one Grand Cru, Wineck-Schlossberg which, with Kaefferkopf, produces superior rieslings, muscats, and gewürztraminers, such as those from Martin Schaetzel. Visit the vine garden and Saint Martin's church, enjoy the April Wine Fair, or join the Vinogast celebration on the second weekend in December.

Continuing down the Route des Vins past Colmar, you arrive at Turkheim, some 4 miles (7 kilometers) south of Colmar.

Considered to produce the best pinot gris in Alsace, it is home to the Grand Cru Brand, which is planted with pinot gris, riesling, and gewürztraminer. Taste the wines at Cave de Turkheim, Zind-Humbrecht, and Meyer. Visit Stork's Park, Sainte-Anne's church with its 1190 belfry porch, the Renaissance town hall, and Hôtel des Deux Clefs. Listen to the town crier at 10:00pm on summer evenings.

Wintzenheim, 2 miles (4 kilometers) west of Colmar, which has one of the most famous terroirs in Alsace, the Grand Cru Hengst, is dominated by the Hohlandsbourg and Pflixbourg castles. Visit Josmeyer, Krick and Schoepfer to taste their wines. Other local attractions include a flower market on the first Saturday in May, a festival on the first weekend in October, and the Christmas market. Follow the scenic route past the area's five castles and the remains of a Gallo-Roman villa on the Hengst slope.

Situated at the foot of the *Trois Châteaux* (three castles) 3 miles (5 kilometers) south of Colmar, is Eguisheim, a medieval city built in three concentric circles around its castle. It is home to the famous Grand Cru vineyards of Eichberg and Pfersigberg, both of which produce fantastic gewürztraminers. Enquire at the tourism office about guided visits and tastings on the vineyard trail, and taste wines at Léon Beyer and Bruno Sorg. Explore the village church with its Roman art, the historic half-timbered houses, tithe manors, and remains of an octagonal Roman castle. A wine growers' festival is held on the fourth weekend of August.

Finally, end your tour at Guebwiller, situated 18 miles (30 kilometers) south of Colmar. This is the only Alsace commune with four Grands Crus: Kessler, Kitterlé, Saering, and Spiegel. Stop and taste wine at Schlumberger. Visit the 14th-century church and former convent (now a musical center), and the 12th-century Saint-Léger's church. A wine fair takes place on Ascension Day.

ALSACE

FAR LEFT Sign on the premises of Hugel, in the main street of Riquewihr, Haut-Rhin.
LEFT A stork nesting on a purpose-made platform in Ribeauvillé, Haut-Rhin.

MAIN GRAPES
White: Gewürztraminer, muscat d'Alsace, pinot blanc, riesling, sylvaner, tokay pinot gris.
Red: Pinot noir.

MAIN WINES (APPELLATIONS)
Alsace, Alsace Grand Cru, Crémant d'Alsace.

MAIN PRODUCERS
Riquewihr: Dopff au Moulin, Hugel & Fils.
Ribeauvillé: Cave Vinicole de Ribeauvillé, Andre Kientzler, Trimbach.
Rouffach: Domaine du Clos Saint-Landelin, Rouffach.
Husseren-les-Châteaux: Kuentz Bas.
Eguisheim: Léon Beyer.
Orschwihr: Lucien Albrecht.
Bergheim: Marcel Deiss.
Epfig: Ostertag.
Kientzheim: Paul Blanck.
Guebwiller: Schlumberger.
Colmar: Schoffit.
Kayserberg: Weinbach-Colette Faller et ses fils.
Turkheim: Zind-Humbrecht.

MAIN TOWNS
Strasbourg, Molsheim, Barr, Sélestat, Ribeauvillé, Colmar, Guebwiller, Thann, Mulhouse.

AIRPORTS
(connections from Paris)
Strasbourg–Entzheim Airport, 9 miles (15km) from Strasbourg; Mulhouse–Bâle (Basel) Airport, 15 miles (25km) from Mulhouse.

TRAINS
Strasbourg, Colmar and Mulhouse.

DAYS
Five.

BEST TIME TO GO
April to December.

SUMMARY
Routes des Vin:
Bas-Rhin (Northern Alsace):
Marlenheim – Dahlenheim – Bergbieten – Wolxheim – Molsheim – Heiligenstein – Barr – Mittelbergheim – Andlau – Nothalten – Dambach-la Ville.
Haut-Rhin (Southern Alsace):
St-Hippolyte – Rodern – Bergheim – Ribeauvillé – Hunawihr – Riquewihr – Mittelwihr – Bennwihr – Kientzheim – Kaysersberg – Sigolsheim – Ammerschwihr – Ingersheim – Colmar – Turkheim – Wintzenheim – Wettolsheim – Eguisheim – Gueberschwihr – Pfaffenheim – Soultzmatt – Rouffach – Westhelten – Orschwihr – Guebwiller – Thann.

SOURCES OF INFORMATION
• *CIVA (Conseil Interprofessionnel des Vins d'Alsace)*
Tel: +33 03.89.20.16.20
Fax: +33 03.89.20.16.30.
Email: civa@civa.fr
Web: www.vinsalsace.com
• *Maison du Tourisme*
Tel: +33 03.89.20.10.68.
Web: www.alsace-info.com

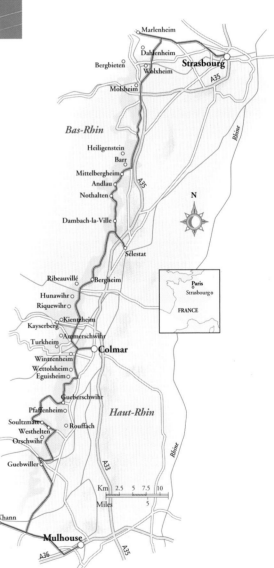

THE MOSEL

GILES MACDONOGH

There are certainly older vineyard sites in Greece, Italy, even France, but the antiquity of the Mosel cannot be denied. Wine has been produced in the valley since the second century AD. We know a lot about those early vineyards from D. Magnus Ausonius's Latin poem 'Mosella.' Ausonius had wine in his blood. He came from another classic wine region, Bordeaux, but nonetheless eulogized the vineyards and sheer slate slopes of the Mosel. He was not wrong. In my opinion, next to the Douro Valley, this is still the loveliest wine region on earth.

It is remarkable that such a northern region should have been so extensively cultivated by the Romans, but it was and is a considerable suntrap. Ausonius pointed out many of the salient features of the vineyards from what was probably only a brief visit: the autumnal mists, which encourage the development of *Botrytis cinerea* or 'noble rot,' and the sweet-smelling vines which rise 700 feet (200 meters) from the banks of the river to the very top of the hillsides and are reflected in the water below. The Mosel guarantees ripeness in the best grapes, which occupy the steep middle band; the top of the slope is never so good; and at the bottom the incline is too gentle to reflect the water and the soil has more loam and pebbles than slate.

The vines were there at the beginning of the seventh century, when Venatius Fortunatus wrote of fruitful cliffs that flowed with wine. By then the Church had become the landlord, and remained so until Napoleon secularized the region. Many of the best estates in the Mosel were once the exclusive domains of monks and bishops. The whole of Zeltingen was a fief of the Archbishop of Cologne, and the growers were his mere share croppers; the Paulinshof in Kesten belonged to the lovely rococo abbey of that name in Trier; Maximin Grünhaus was once part of the Benedictine Abbey of Saint Maximin in the same city; and the Karthäuserhof down the road was there to provide moral support for the silent Carthusians. Those are just a few examples.

LEFT Mist lingers on riesling vines in the Würzgarten vineyard, high above the Mosel at Ürzig. The Roman poet Ausonius was the first to record this climatic phenomenon in the second century AD.

The monks of Saint Maximin and the Carthusians both favored the banks of the Ruwer, just outside the Roman city of Trier, where, in Ausonius's time, imported marble was cut for building. Any tour should begin in this fascinating city, with its substantial remains of the amphitheater, the Porta Nigra, and the magnificent cathedral, or Dom.

Two south-facing vineyards excel here: the Karthäuserhofberg, property of the Tyrell family, with its iron-rich red slate; and the blue slate Abtsberg, which is exclusive to Maximin Grünhaus. Splendid wines are also to be had from Maximin Grünhaus's red slate Herrenberg and from the Nieschen slope in neighboring Kasel. Both Maximin Grün-haus and the Karthäuserhof retain relics of their past. In the 19th century, the former's buildings were turned into a baronial estate for the Kaiser's friend, von Stumm-Halberg, an ancestor of the present owners, the von Schuberts. The witty decor of the billiard room at the Karthäuserhof, which is used for tastings, also dates from the Kaiser's time.

The Ruwer feeds the Mosel as that river treads its tortuous path, snaking its way round rock and cliff on its way to meet the Rhine at Koblenz. There are good villages in the southern section of the Middle Mosel and also some famous vineyard sites, such as the Apotheke (Apothecary) in Trittenheim – a glass of wine from here was thought to be an efficient pick-me-up when the Moselaners felt under the weather.

The next village is Piesport, which enjoys worldwide fame. But while a real Piesporter

ABOVE The highly rated Goldtröpfchen vineyard rises behind the town of Piesport. Goldtröpfchen, which means 'little drop of gold,' makes some of the best wines in the Mosel valley.

LEFT Erden's 'Sonnenuhr,' or sundial, vineyard is situated in one of the valley's steepest yet sunniest spots.

OPPOSITE Bernkastel and its wall of vineyards, as seen from the Burg Landshut. The minuscule Doctor vineyard, to the left of the town, is probably the most famous vineyard site in Germany.

from a great year is a wonderful experience, beware of the all-embracing appellation, or *Grosslage*, Piesporter Michelsberg, as no great wine is sold as such. (*Grosslage* means a large site, or a collection of individual sites.) The best vineyard here is the Goldtröpfchen, a reference to the color and value of the wines that it produces. A reliable producer is Reichsgraf von Kesselstatt, based in Trier.

At Brauneberg the Mosel enters its most star-studded stretch. Powerful, gutsy wines come from the Paulinshofberg, with its bronze and grey slates. A Roman presshouse, discovered here, has been restored. The most famous Brauneberg vineyards are Juffer and

Juffer Sonnenuhr. Juffer is a corruption of *Jungfer* (maiden), a reference to the unmarried daughters of the Elector's chamberlains who possessed a convent here and had substantial vineyard holdings before Napoleon upset the apple-cart in 1803. As local grower Dirk Richter puts it: 'It's the only virgin that improves with age.' Fortuitously, perhaps, the wines from Brauneberg are supposed to be slightly feminine, where those of Wehlen, say, are distinctly manly. The names to conjure with here are Fritz Haag and Max Ferd Richter, but at Schloss Lieser, Haag's son Thomas is also proving to be a chip off the old block with some very fine, elegant Mosels.

Europe's largest vineyard is the unbroken 5 mile (8 kilometer) wall which stretches from Bernkastel to Zeltingen. Bernkastel is the Mosel's hub. It is riddled with tourists, and the shops seem to cater for them alone. From here you may catch a boat to admire the vines from the water, or rent a bicycle to race along the cycle tracks up in the vines along with the stout German pensioners who like to spend their holidays doing just that.

The evenings, of course, should be spent mulling over a bottle, or two, of Mosel wine. Local inns offer *gutbürgerliche Küche* (honest, plain cooking) along with wines that come from the best slopes of the valley. You should, however, take care. The soil alone can't make the wine, and unless the grapes have been carefully grown and meticulously vinified, the wine will not impress. Always stick to a known name if you can.

Bernkastel is home to some of the best vineyards, including the legendary Doctor, whose wine could treat a patient; and the wonderful Alte Badstube am Doctorberg next door, property of Dr. Pauly Bergweiler.

The lyrical names of the vineyards north of Bernkastel used to make our forefathers salivate and, a century ago, a good Mosel fetched a far higher price than it does today. Names to look out for include Graacher or Zeltinger Himmelreich (both villages, you see, own a chunk of *himmel*, or heaven), Wehlener Sonnenuhr (one of the Mosel's famous 'sundial' vineyards which catch the most heat), Ürziger Würzgarten (the 'spice garden' which produces wines that seem to taste of cinnamon), Erdener Prälat (the 'bishop') and Treppchen (or 'little steps,' after a rocky feature at the heart of the vineyard).

Willi Schaefer makes a divine Graacher Himmelreich from his tiny estate; Selbach Oster is great for his Graacher Domprobst (named for a former dean of the cathedral, as the wines were once a gift of the deanery), and the Zeltener Sonnenuhr.

The name on everybody's lips when it comes to Wehlener Sonnenuhr is J.J. Prüm. These vineyards are now owned by Manfred Prüm, whose lovely Art Nouveau house is on the other side of the river with a perfect view towards the jewel in his crown. Prüms crop up all over the Mosel; it is even the name of one of the tributaries of the river, so it helps to know who's who.

The Prüms always reigned in Wehlen, just as the Berres family controlled Ürzig, the Thanisches ruled in Bernkastel (where they own a part of the legendary Doctor vineyard), and the Richters in the Protestant enclave of Mülheim. Noteworthy wines also come from Dr. Loosen in Wehlen, who is recommended for a further three sites: Erdener Treppchen, Erdener Prälat, and Ürziger Würzgarten.

All these men travel around the world selling their wines, so it can be hard to meet them. Often you must be content with the wine itself, perhaps drunk in a local restaurant or hotel.

The wines of the Lower Mosel, closer to Koblenz, rarely achieve the same levels of sublimity, but there are good things to be had from sites like the Ennkircher Batterieberg. Traben Trarbach is one of the region's more attractive towns. Particularly recommended is the Art Nouveau Hotel Bellevue, designed by the architect Bruno Möhring.

BELOW Trittenheim, seen from the Klostergarten, lies within an ox-bow bend in the Mosel. The flat land beyond the river makes very ordinary wine.

THE MOSEL

MAIN GRAPES White: Riesling.

LEADING VILLAGES AND PRODUCERS
(*Leading vineyards in brackets*).
Saar: Schloss Saarstein, Bert Simon.
Ruwer: Maximin Grünhaus (Abtsberg, Herrenberg), Karthäuserhof.
Trittenheim: (Apotheke).
Piesport: Reichsgraf von Kesselstatt (Goldtröpfchen).
Brauneberg: Fritz Haag (Juffer, Juffer Sonnenuhr).
Kesten: Paulinshof (Paulinshofberg).
Mülheim: Max Ferd Richter.
Lieser: Schloss Lieser.
Bernkastel: Dr. Pauly Bergweiler, Dr. Loosen (Doctor, Alte Badstube am Doctorberg).
Zeltingen: Selbach-Oster (Himmelreich).
Graach: Willi Schaefer (Himmelreich, Domprobst).
Wehlen: J.J. Prüm (Sonnenuhr).
Ürzig: Dr. Loosen (Würzgarten).
Erden: Dr. Loosen (Prälat, Treppchen).
Enkirch: (Batterieberg).

MAIN TOWNS Trier, Bernkastel, Koblenz.

AIRPORT Frankfurt (Hahn) – 30 minutes.

DAYS Three.

BEST TIME TO GO June to October.

SUMMARY Trier – Saar – Ruwer – Piesport – Bernkastel – Traben-Trarbach – Koblenz.

SOURCES OF INFORMATION
• *Moselandtouristik*, Gestade 12–14, Postfach 1310, 54470 Bernkastel-Kues.
Tel: +49 (6531) 2091
Fax: +49 (6531) 2093.
• *German Wine Institute, Mainz*
Tel: +49 (6131) 28290
Fax: +49 (6131) 282-920.
Web: www.deutscheweine.de

THE RHEINGAU

GILES MACDONOGH

The Rheingau is small; just a 20-mile (32-kilometer) strip. Protected from the north by the Taunus mountains, it faces due south across one of the widest stretches of the Rhine. The combination of mostly slate soils and intense sunlight reflected off the waters of the river combine to ripen riesling grapes to perfection, which is not normal above the 50th parallel – here grapes are not supposed to ripen at all.

The Rheingau is the great inventor, and much of what is significant in the development of German wine occurred here first. As with many other wine-producing regions, it was the church that developed the former Roman vineyards. The Benedictines created the wines of Johannisberg, while their austere reformed wing, the Cistercians, installed themselves in the damp valley of Eberbach, but were careful to plant their grapes on the sunniest slopes around.

Those first wines were probably mostly red – what the Germans call Burgunder – members of the pinot family: noir, gris and blanc. How good they were is disputed now; all we know is that the riesling grape gradually took over, spreading first from Hochheim, where it is mentioned as early as the 15th century, to the rest of the valley. It was successfully introduced as a single variety in Johannisberg in the 1720s, and the way was open to replace the pinots.

Kloster Eberbach and Johannisberg dispute the invention of wine affected by 'noble rot.' A document of 1753 from Eberbach calls the 'rotten grapes ... the best.' At Johannisberg they made the first nobly rotten 'Spätlese' in 1775 when the Abbot of Fulda was famously late in giving the go-ahead for picking. (That 'Spätlese' was almost certainly what the 1971 Wine Law would call an Auslese or above.) The idea of picking *Botrytis cinerea*-affected grapes rapidly caught on after that. The first Auslese was also made at Johannisberg in the 1780s. At Kloster Eberbach the notion of 'Kabinett' first saw the light of day in 1730, when the best wines were

LEFT A small wayfarers' chapel divides the Schönhell (bright light) and Würzgarten (spice garden) vineyards in the Rheingau village of Hallgarten. Some of Germany's best riesling wines come from these slopes.

kept back in the Kabinett-Keller. These were more carefully vinified, and could be sold as mature wines when a cold summer meant they had insufficient wine to sell. A similar system evolved at Schloss Vollrads. At Kloster Eberbach you may taste a wine which is made in the style of the first Kabinetts. It is a powerful, half-dry Auslese.

Rheingau wine means 'hock,' which derives from 'Hochheimer.' In the 19th century these highly selective 'hocks' were considered to be among the best wines in the world, with prices easily trouncing the first growths of Bordeaux. One of the most famous, an 1893 Auslese from Robert Weil, was served at the table of the last German Kaiser.

In recent years there has been an occasionally acrimonious debate as to whether the traditional hock was sweet or dry. The answer is somewhere between the two. As people didn't know how to stop the fermentation artificially, and because the wines lay in cask for over a year before they were bottled, they fermented out more than wines do today. In good years, however, they probably had many more than 10 grams per liter residual sugar. They would have been

bigger, more powerful wines than either the little sweeties of the 1950s and 1960s or the austerely dry wines which were all the rage in the 1980s. However, the great Auslesen, Beerenauslesen and Trockenbeerenauslesen wines were all naturally sweet.

Hochheim is just 15 minutes from Frankfurt airport, on the way to Wiesbaden and Mainz. It is the natural and historical beginning to a tour. What was formerly little more than a village has now become a suburban town, but the historic core is sound and the hot, contained island of vines that rises from the River Main is vigorously defended against the developers. A delight is the Königin Victoria Berg, with its little monument celebrating Queen Victoria's visit in 1850. It is a charming spot for a picnic. Bring a bottle of wine and salute the trains that hoot at revelers as they whistle past.

Two estates in Hochheim vie for attention. The first, Domdechant Werner, is owned by traditionalist Dr. Michel whose charming Biedermeyer house overlooks the vineyards. Most of his wines contain residual sugar although they are so wonderfully balanced you would hardly know. Opposite is

Gunter Künstler, the 'new broom,' a dynamic figure whose father came to Hochheim after the war as a refugee from Nikolsburg in German-speaking Moravia. His wines have plenty of body, but are almost always dry. Hochheimer wines have a certain earthiness about them in general, which is not generally found in the rest of the Rheingau.

Erbach is 20 minutes' drive from Hochheim. Here is Schloss Reinhartshausen, once owned by a branch of the Prussian royal family which attracted a deal of scandal in its day. The mansion is now a Relais & Châteaux hotel with two fine, if expensive, restaurants looking out over the Rhine. The estate makes wine in some of the best vineyard sites of all, including the magnificent Marcobrunn, which lies just behind the Schloss.

The best estate in Kiedrich is Robert Weil, which produces superlative wines from the southwest-facing Gräfenberg. The estate was founded in 1871 after Weil was compelled to give up his teaching post at the Sorbonne as a result of the Franco-German war. He settled in a half-timbered house built by English baronet Sir John Sutton, who was responsible for restoring the village's magnificent church.

Weil added to the house, but the original design remains. Sutton died in Bruges in 1873, but his tomb is in the churchyard up the road.

Kloster Eberbach is in Hallgarten, near the village of Hattenheim. Here, in 1136, the Cistercians established their first monastery on the right bank of the Rhine. In 1803 French invaders plundered the interiors and destroyed the cloister, but the rest, happily, is in a great state of preservation, including the bare, Romanesque church and the rococo dining room dating from 1738.

After 1815, Kloster Eberbach became the Staatsweingut (state winery) of Hessen. In 1866, when war broke out between Austria and Prussia, the royal family of Hessen sided with Austria, which was defeated. As a result, Prussia annexed Hessen, and the Prussian eagle soon appeared on bottles from the Staatsweingut. The eagle is still there (despite the fact that the Staatsweingut reverted to the modern Land Hessen in 1947,) but has become rather limp in recent years, in an attempt to make it look more friendly.

The Staatsweingut Hessen is the biggest estate in Germany. Its total of 468 acres (194 hectares) includes large tracts of vineyard outside the Rheingau, on the Bergstrasse, plus about 74 acres (30 hectares) of Spätburgunder (pinot noir) in Assmannshausen. One of its finest vineyards is the walled Steinberg, which year in, year out makes lovely wines.

Nearby Hattenheim is one of the many fiefs of the powerful Schönborn family. They have 123 acres (50 hectares) of vines here, more a long way away in Franconia, and own the fantastic baroque Schloss Weissenfels in Pommersfelden, near Bamberg in Franconia. Many of the present count's ancestors were princes of the Church. A cousin is currently Cardinal Archbishop of Vienna. The wines are among the most traditional in the Rheingau. Nearby is Zum Krug, the best restaurant around in which to drink old hocks.

In Oestrich is the fine old Hotel Schwan, where the rooms look out over the Rhine. The most famous estate is Schloss Vollrads which, until recently, was owned by the Greiffenclau family, one of the oldest in Europe. Wine has been made here since the ninth century, and sold since the 13th. The Greiffenclaus kept a library of precious books in the old water tower, and they lived in a sumptuous schloss. In the pond below the tower, ancient carp and turtles bask in the sun. The wines, however, were often mean and lean, and the family hit hard times. There has been a change of heart since the bank took over and the wines have become more generous – odd, for a bank.

Another distinguished Oestrich grower is Peter Jakob Kühn, who owns chunks of Lendchen and the Doosberg. He is a perfectionist who lavishes attention on every one of his vines. Occasionally he opens his house to what is known as a *Strausswirtschaft*; growers serve food and their own wines to anyone who is ready to pay. His wife cooks ham in riesling, served with a Rheingauer sauce made of seven herbs, milk, and chopped eggs. It was a favorite of the poet Goethe, who came from nearby Frankfurt.

Rüdesheim was badly damaged in the war, but you would hardly know it now. It can be forbiddingly touristy, with the hotels and restaurants filled with cheerful visitors doing the chicken dance, making it hard to imagine people being serious about wine. One man who is deeply earnest about his winemaking, however, is Georg Breuer, who has built up a large estate in the best and steepest sites, situated on dark blue slate, high above the town, from where he makes very powerful dry wines. Sweet wines are the exception here, but when Breuer makes them, they are extremely good.

Another star winemaker in Rüdesheim is Johannes Leitz, who farms the perilously steep slopes beneath the Niederwald, a huge monument to German victory in the 1870–71 war against France. It is emblazoned with the words of the nationalist hymn 'Die Wacht am Rhein,' and some local people are clearly embarrassed by its prominence. However, Leitz has other concerns. He likes to repeat the old maxim about planting: if a horse can stand upright, the land is not right for vines.

Round the corner from Rüdesheim is Assmannshausen, a small surviving pocket of Spätburgunder (pinot noir) vines in the Rheingau. The main producer is the Staatsweingut Hessen. The wines are traditionally made in old oak casks. In good years they taste like light, red burgundy. The sparkling version was the favorite wine of Kaiser William, who drank a glass with his meals until his death in exile in Holland in 1941.

BELOW Assmannshausen is the home of Germany's most famous red wine, made from pinot noir; the steep Höllenberg vineyard is the village's best site.

LEFT Made from sheep's milk, pecorino cheese is perfect with Tuscan wines. The best pecorino, from Pienza, can be enjoyed when it is either young and creamy or mature and tangy.

MAIN TOWNS Montalcino,
Montepulciano, Siena, Florence.

AIRPORTS Siena, Florence.

DAYS Five.

BEST TIME TO GO
April to November. May: *Cantine Aperte* –
many local wineries are officially open to
the public during this event; September:
Montalcino Honey Festival;
Montepulciano Vin Santo and Donut
(*ciambellina*) Festival.

SUMMARY
Montalcino and Montepulciano.
Those with additional time may wish to
visit Siena and Florence, as well as the
Chianti zone which lies between them.
Northeast of Siena, the hilltop town of
San Gimignano is the center of Vernaccia
di San Gimignano DOCG production.

SOURCES OF INFORMATION
• *Consorzio del Vino Brunello di Montalcino*
Costa del Municipio 1, 53024 Montalcino, Italy.
Tel: +39 (577) 848246
Fax: +39 (577) 849425.
Email: consbrun@tin.it
Web: www.consorziobrunellodimontalcino.it
• *Consorzio del Vino Nobile di Montepulciano*
Piazza Grande 7, 53045 Montepulciano, Italy.
Tel: +39 (578) 757-812
Fax: +39 (578) 758-213.
Email: nobile@bccmp.com
Web: www.vinonobiledimontepulciano.it

MAIN GRAPES
Red: Sangiovese.
White: Vernaccia di San Gimignano.

LEADING WINES (DOC/DOCG zones):
Brunello di Montalcino, Vino Nobile di
Montepulciano, Chianti, Chianti Classico,
Carmignano, Morellino di Scansano, Bolgheri,
Vernaccia di San Gimignano.

MAIN PRODUCERS
(*The following are just a sample of the many producers
of fine Brunello and Vino Nobile. Do not hesitate to try
wines from other estates.*)
Brunello di Montalcino: Altesino, Biondi-Santi,
Fattoria dei Barbi, Camigliano, Tenuta Caparzo,
Col d'Orcia, Lisini, Poggio Antico, Villa Banfi,
Tenuta il Poggione, Mastrojanni.
Vino Nobile di Montepulciano: Avignonesi,
Boscarelli, Poliziano, Salcheto, Tenimenti Angelini,
Bindella, Fattoria del Cerro, Fassati, La Calonica,
Vecchia Cantina di Montepulciano.

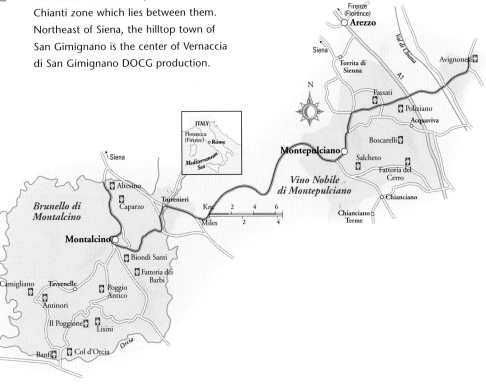

ITALY

VENETO

PATRICIA GUY

First-time visitors to the Veneto tend to head straight for the decadent delights of Venice, but the elegant charms of Verona, just over an hour away, have more to offer the wine traveler. Set below the foothills of the Alps in a gentle curve of the Adige River, Verona is noted for its thriving Romeo and Juliet industry, thousand-year-old Roman arena (a summer venue for internationally renowned opera performances), and its unparalleled position as the center of the Veneto's wine country. Well over half the region's wines, classified as DOC (*Denominazione di Origine Controllata*) and DOCG (*Denominazione di Origine Controllata e Garantita*, a higher classification), are produced in the province of Verona, and it is these wines – Amarone, Valpolicella, Bardolino, and Soave – which have shaped the region's international identity.

After a quick cappuccino at any of the pleasant cafés in the historic center of Verona (and there is at least one on every street), it will be time to set out for your first day trip. Some 40 minutes' drive to the west of the city will bring you to Bardolino on the shore of Lago di Garda (Lake Garda), Italy's largest lake. The town, which lends its name to the wine zone, is an attractive collection of chic beachwear shops and good, casual restaurants and wine bars clustered around the marina. Boats set out regularly to ferry visitors around the vast expanse of the lake, whose shores lie within three regions, the Veneto on the east bank, Lombardy on the west bank, and a bit of Trentino at the northern tip.

The fossilized remains of grape leaves and bunches found in this zone testify to its long grape-growing history, and records show that wine has been made here since at least the start of the first millennium. Production is dominated by three grape varieties, corvina, rondinella and molinara, which are blended to produce Bardolino, a fresh, light, and attractive dry red. They are also used in the production of Valpolicella and Amarone, the area's other fine reds.

LEFT The vineyards around the town of Bardolino benefit from the reflection of the sun's rays off Lago di Garda. Take a walk among the vineyards of the *strada del vino* (wine road), sampling local olive oil and wine.

Bardolino comes in a variety of styles, including a lively rosé (Chiaretto), which the locals consider a perfect accompaniment to trout. A fuller-bodied, more structured style, Bardolino Superiore, has the distinction of being the Veneto's first DOCG red wine. The DOCG is the highest accolade offered by the Italian government and is intended to serve as a guarantee of quality.

With their cherry-tinged fruit and zippy acidity, these wines are fine accompaniments to local specialties such as *bigoli con l'agole* (thick spaghetti served with whitebait), *carne salada* (salted raw beef), and *risotto alla tinca* (risotto with tench, a local freshwater fish).

The estates of all the best producers are within a short drive or, in some cases, stroll of the town. Directions can be obtained from the local tourist bureau or the Bardolino Consortium, located in Piazza Matteotti, the town's main square. A few miles outside Bardolino, at Cisano on the road back to

ABOVE Marano di Valpolicella is an unspoilt hillside village that produces many of the denomination's most elegant wines.

RIGHT The majestic castle of Soave, venue for concerts, theatrical performances, and 'medieval' pageantry, dominates the DOC zone's vineyards.

Verona, you will find the olive oil museum. Stop in for a taste of the rich fruity oil that is justly famous.

The Valpolicella zone lies to the east of Bardolino. Its natural boundaries are the Lessini mountains to the north and the Veronese plain to the south, with the Soave zone to the east and the Adige River to the west. Some of its vineyards date back to the Bronze Age and scientists believe that grapes have been vinified here on a regular basis since the eighth century BC.

Valpolicellas range from simple, dry, and refreshing reds intended for early drinking to the fuller, richer single-vineyard wines, which have a longer aging potential. The supple body and plummy/cherry fruit flavor of Valpolicella make it a good match for a delicious local *sopressa* (salami), and it goes equally well with pasta in meat sauce. Fuller-bodied versions can even be paired with Veronese specialties such as *pastissada di caval* (horsemeat stew) and *bigoli con l'anatra* (thick spaghetti with duck ragout).

TUSCANY

MONTALCINO AND MONTEPULCIANO

PATRICIA GUY

The 'idea' of Tuscany, that story-book landscape where elegant walled cities crown every hilltop, and fields, vineyards, and orchards are arranged in burnished rectangles as neat as the patterns of your grandmother's quilt, has entered into the fantasies of day-dreamers everywhere. And the region does, indeed, live up to its reputation. However, those distant fortress-towns tell a story filled with passion and power that has little to do with fairy tales. Their austere beauty is a reminder of the centuries-long struggle for power fought between the cities of Florence and Siena. As each city sought to gain control of the surrounding territories, the populace moved to the defensive positions that the hilltops offered. The constant shifting of allegiances affected not only Tuscany's history and culture but also its viticulture, all of which combine great refinement with hard-headed pragmatism.

Tuscany's winemaking evolution is quite unlike that of other parts of Italy. Here wine production has always been linked with the fortunes of the nobility. In his 1833 classic, *The History and Description of Modern Wines*, Cyrus Redding writes of Florentine nobles who 'sell their wine by retail from their palace cellars ... without any excess, all the classes in Tuscany enjoy their wine, fancying it makes good blood.'

During the mid-1800s Baron Bettino Ricasoli began experimenting with local grape varieties on his family estate in Chianti. The Iron Baron, as Ricasoli was known, subsequently established the sangiovese-based recipe for Chianti wine that became part of Italy's DOC laws. In 1870, the baron became prime minister of Italy and, for a brief time, Florence was the capital of the newly united nation. The families of Antinori, Frescobaldi, Mazzei (of Castello di Fonterutoli) and

LEFT Many Tuscan estates, like the Swiss-owned Vallocaia near Montepulciano, have been purchased by non-Italians who have been entranced by the region's vineyards, olive groves, and rich cultural heritage.

Medici (related to the current owners of Badia a Coltibuono) are among the nobility who, through centuries, shaped the destiny of the Chianti zone and, indeed, of Tuscany itself.

First-time visitors to the region flock to Florence and then, perhaps, take the winding road to Siena, stopping at their favorite Chianti Classico estates on the way. This tour of Tuscany will take you a little further south, to two beautiful and historic hilltop towns, Montepulciano and Montalcino, which were pawns in the game of power played by Siena and Florence. Both produce sangiovese-based wines that boast the DOCG (*Denominazione*

di Origine Controllata e Garantita), Italy's most prestigious quality designation; notably Vino Nobile di Montepulciano and Brunello di Montalcino (long one of the world's most powerful and sought-after wines).

The town of Montepulciano rises from the crest of a volcanic hill between the Chiana and Orcia valleys. It was mentioned for the first time as Monte Politianus in a document dating from AD715. Very little ancient architecture remains; rather, the austere stone buildings give a glimpse of Gothic and Renaissance grandeur. For a time, the town enjoyed the patronage of the

Medici family, which commissioned works by the finest architects and artists. The tower in Piazza Grande, Montepulciano's main square, offers a stunning view over the town and the vine-clad hillsides which surround it.

As beautiful and compelling as it is, Montepulciano hides its most seductive side, at least as far as the winelover is concerned. Carved from the volcanic rock under the town is a vast network of caves and passages, which was essential to the town's survival and, for a time, served as a secret winery. Throughout the ongoing wars between Siena and Florence, the strategic stronghold of

RIGHT Montalcino is the center of a zone that produces not only a rich, full-bodied red, but also a luscious dessert wine, Moscadello di Montalcino.

BELOW RIGHT The tasting room of the Avignonesi estate, producer of fine Vino Nobile and Rosso di Montepulciano, as well as exquisite Vin Santo.

OPPOSITE The hilltop town of Montepulciano has breathtaking views over vineyards and olive groves. Local shops sell wines, cheese, and oils of the region.

Montepulciano was frequently under siege. Its citizens took refuge in these caves and at harvest time, rather than risk losing the crop, they brought their grapes here to vinify and store them. Until well into the 20th century, estates in the zone continued to use the town's cellars for aging their vino nobile.

To understand the full extent of this wondrous achievement, visit the Cantina del Redi, which lies under the Palazzo Ricci. The high-vaulted ceilings of volcanic stone are breathtaking, and a walk through the narrow carved passages gives the wine lover a real understanding of the history, the tragedy, and the passion that great wine can engender.

Vino Nobile di Montepulciano gained its 'nobility' in the 18th century. It is believed that the designation 'nobile' was used to indicate wine that was a cut above the ordinary and therefore suitable for noblemen who could pay a higher price. Another theory suggests that the 'nobile' comes from the fact that many local noblemen were producers.

Modern Vino Nobile is made from a minimum of 70 percent sangiovese (a sub-variety known as prugnolo gentile), with the option of adding other approved red grape varieties, among these canaiolo nero. The wine is aged for two years before being released. It has a deep, dense ruby color and a spicy, plummy, ever-evolving flavor.

Winemakers suggest that this elegant and complex red wine be served with such local specialities as *i pici al ragu* (handmade pasta

with a rich meat sauce), *bistecca chianina* (T-bone steak), *arrosto misto* (assorted roast meats) and *peposo* (beef slowly braised in red wine and seasoned with peppercorns).

Montalcino, at the confluence of the Orcia and Ombrone rivers was, like Montepulciano, the site of intense disputes between the warring city-states of Florence and Siena. Many buildings in this walled city belong to the Renaissance, with the exception of the 14th-century Palazzo Pubblico and the castle, from whose ramparts can be seen a grand, undulating sweep of vines.

Decent wine had been produced on these hillsides since the Middle Ages, but in the mid-1800s, fate, in the person of Clemente Santi, stepped in and forever altered the fortunes of the town and its wine. Clemente Santi's Vino Rosso Scelto far outshone other wines from its district, even winning top honors at exhibitions in London and Paris. Ferruccio Biondi Santi, Clemente's grandson, set about identifying and isolating the local mutation of the sangiovese grape which gave his grandfather's wines their exceptional concentration of fruit. This mutation, or clone, was named Brunello di Montalcino to distinguish it from other sangiovese vines. In 1964, Ferruccio's son, Tancredi, assisted in drawing up the DOC production regulations for the Brunello di Montalcino zone.

Brunello's production zone is limited to the commune of Montalcino in the province of Siena. The wine is deep ruby-red, tending towards garnet with age. Its perfumes are rich and full. Tasters find hints of leather, tobacco, truffles, figs, mulberries, raspberries, vanilla, and cinnamon on the nose.

In the past, there have been claims that the wine could age for 50 years or more and it was considered unapproachable for at least 10 years. However, contemporary Brunello producers have followed the example set in other fine wine zones, such as Bordeaux, and now vinify their wines in a way that makes them ready to drink shortly after release, even if they will improve with cellaring.

Brunello's rich and mouth-filling fruit calls for aromatic and flavorful dishes, such as braised or stewed red meats. Locals serve it with *scottiglia di coniglio* (pan-grilled rabbit) or *cinghiale* (wild boar).

Both zones also produce lighter DOC wines, which are usually made from younger vines and have shorter aging periods. Rosso di Montepulciano and Rosso di Montalcino tend to be livelier, easier to drink and much less expensive than their DOCG brothers.

The next time you taste a glass of Brunello, Vino Nobile or Chianti, appreciate the subtle differences of style of which sangiovese, one of Italy's great grape varieties, is capable. It is attempting to capture these elusive nuances that makes wine-tasting such a wonderful and sensuous experience.

LEFT Immaculately tended plots of Brunello vines (also known as sangiovese grosso), surround the 15th-century palazzo, cypress grove, and stables at the Altesino estate in Montalcino.

Brunn-im-Felde lies on the eastern side of Krems. The most notable wine producer here is Sepp Mantler, who is best known for vinifying the spicy roter veltliner (a dark-skinned green grape – black grapes are called *blau*, or blue, in German). He also makes wonderful grüner veltliners at all levels of ripeness from Kabinett (dry) to Trockenbeerenauslese (late harvest-sweet).

On the way back to Krems you pass Rohrendorf, the home of producer Lenz Moser. This large firm is no longer in family hands, but Sepp Moser, the brother of the last Lenz to own the company, produces some of Austria's very best chardonnays: wonderfully unwooded from Ried Gebling, and subtly oaked from Ried Schnabel, both with a steely seam of acidity. ('Ried' means vineyard.)

The Kremstal region continues across the river, below Göttweig monastery. Here the most notable grower is Gerald Malat, a former skiing instructor and motor racer with a fondness for modern technology. A dab hand at the regional classics (grüner veltiner and riesling), Malat is also one of Austria's most convincing exponents of international cultivars, including chardonnay, pinot noir, and Bordeaux blends.

From Furth it is just a short hop to the Wachau and the former Roman town of Mautern on the Danube. The town possesses one of Austria's best restaurants, Bacher. It has rooms too, but book in advance if you plan to stay. The best grower in Mautern is Nikolaus Saahs at the Nikolaihof, where the wines are elegant and long-lasting, and which operates a restaurant for about half the year. Saahs also owns a portion of the Steiner Hund in Krems.

The Wachau's densest wines come from Loiben, across the river. The village is split into Unter- and Oberloiben, and sports a concentration of fine growers, and a good restaurant, the Loibnerhof, which is owned by Josef Knoll. Emmerich Knoll, his cousin, is one of Austria's half-dozen best winemakers.

Growers in the Wachau use their own system to grade their sappy, dry white wines, and these names are reflected on the labels. Steinfeder (named for a wispy local plant) is a light unchaptalized summer wine, made for early drinking; Federspiel (falcon) is a Kabinett of medium body; and Smaragd (a local green salamander) is a powerful, dry Kabinett or Spätlese with high alcohol levels. Knoll's Smaragde are always among the richest and most complex wines in the valley.

Knoll's chief rival in Loiben is F.X. Pichler, or 'FX' as he is familiarly known. His wines may lack the opulence of Knoll's, but they are astonishingly multifaceted and exquisitely constructed.

A little further upriver is Dürnstein, a picture-postcard town with its majestic schloss (now a Relais & Châteaux hotel), blue church tower, and the ruined castle, where in the 12th century, Richard the Lionheart was held captive by the Duke of Austria while

LEFT Baroque angels on Dürnstein's church look out over the waters of the Danube – sadly more often red-brown than blue.

past when they were rewarded for their toils. His loveliest wine, however, was a Weissburgunder, which is no longer made.

Weissenkirchen is another lovely town. Its best grower, Toni Bodenstein, makes wine for his father-in-law, Franz Prager. There is a lot more riesling here than is usually the case, and full-bodied Smaragde from Achleiten or Steinriegl have been known to cause Saul-style conversions among sceptikal critics.

In Wösendorf is the upwardly mobile Rudi Pichler – one of many growers of that name in the area. His wines are to some degree typical of the western end of the Wachau, being a shade lighter than those from Loiben, although it should be stressed that they are no wimps: try a grüner veltliner Smaragd from Hochrain and see.

The two leading growers of Spitz, Franz Hirtzberger and Josef Högl, are among Austria's best. Hirtzberger is always spoken of in the same breath as 'FX' Pichler, another star of the Wachau, whose wines are regarded as some of the loveliest dry whites in the world.

Josef Högl's talents were first recognized a decade ago, when it seemed as if the Wachau's old guard would never be toppled by a younger generation. The Pichlers, Pragers, Knolls and Hitzbergers are still there, but there is new blood flowing alongside, with winemakers like Högl producing exemplary grüner veltliner and riesling year in, year out, especially from the Riede Schön and Bruck.

Finish your tour across the river at Melk, with a visit to the most magnificent baroque monastery in Austria.

returning from the third Crusade. The town is also the seat of the biggest local cooperative, the Freie Weingärtner, which makes some fine wines, as well as a mass-marketed blend called Katzensprung, or Cat's Leap. The most eccentric grower in Dürnstein is Franz Schmidl,

the baker, who has achieved international recognition for his *Laiberl* or little loaves. On the wine side, he makes powerful grüner veltliners and rieslings, especially those from the vineyard called Küss den Pfenning (kiss the penny), an expression the casual day workers used in the

MAIN GRAPES

Wachau: Grüner veltliner, müller-thurgau (a riesling sylvaner cross), riesling, neuburger, chardonnay (*feinburgunder*). Small amounts of black grapes, of which zweigelt is the most widely planted type.
Kremstal: Grüner veltliner, less riesling and müller-thurgau than in Wachau. Local specialties such as roter veltliner. Interesting experiments with pinot noir and cabernet sauvignon.

LEADING VILLAGES AND PRODUCERS

WACHAU

Loiben: F.X. Pichler, Emmerich Knoll.
Weissenkirchen: Prager.
Wösendorf: Rudi Pichler.
Spitz: Hirtzberger, Högl.
Mautern: Nikolaihof.

KREMSTAL

Krems: Salomon, Walzer.
Senftenberg: Nigl, Proidl.
Brunn-im-Felde: Mantlerhof.
Rohrendorf-bei-Krems:
Sepp Moser.
Furth-bei-Göttweig: Malat.

MAIN TOWNS Krems-Stein,
Dürnstein, Weissenkirchen.

AIRPORT Vienna (Schwechat), between 60 and 90 minutes from Krems.

LEFT Grüner veltliner vines. Despite riesling's reputation, veltliner can make stunning wine on the best soil.
RIGHT A Loiben grower uses an old barrel-end to advertise his wares to passers-by. Although grüner veltliner and riesling dominate production, Wachau winemakers have a variety of grapes to choose from.

DAYS Three.

BEST TIME TO GO For sunny weather: June to September; to avoid tourists: May or October.

SUMMARY Krems – Senftenberg – Brunn-im-Felde – Rohrendorf-bei-Krems – Göttweig – Mautern – Loiben – Dürnstein – Weissenkirchen – Spitz – Melk.

SOURCES OF INFORMATION
ÖWM (Austrian Wine Marketing Service)
Tel: +43 (1) 587-47670.

THE RHEINGAU

Main grapes

White: Riesling.
Red: Pinot noir (Spätburgunder).

Leading villages and producers

(Leading vineyards in brackets.)
Hochheim: Domdechant Werner, Gunter Künstler.
Erbach: Staatsweingut Eltville, Schloss Reinhartshausen (Marcobrunn).
Kiedrich: Robert Weil (Gräfenberg).
Hattenheim: Schloss Schönborn, Schloss Johannisberg.
Hallgarten: Staatsweingut Hessen.
Oestrich: Schloss Vollrads, Peter Jakob Kühn (Lenchen, Doosberg).

Rüdesheim: Georg Breuer, Johannes Leitz.
Assmannshausen: Staatsweingut Hessen (Höllenberg).

Main towns
Wiesbaden, Mainz, Rüdesheim.

Airport
Frankfurt (30 minutes).

Days
Two.

Best time to go
June to October.

Summary
Hochheim – Erbach – Kiedrich – Hattenheim – Oestrich – Rüdesheim – Assmannshausen.

LEFT The Drosselhof is a pub in the Drosselgasse, the busiest street in Rüdesheim.
CENTER At the heart of Robert Weil's property in Kiedrich is the original home of Sir John Sutton.
RIGHT The former Cistercian monastery of Kloster Eberbach in Hallgarten is the headquarters of the Staatsweingut Hessen.

Sources of Information
• *German Wine Institute*
Tel/Fax: +49 (6131) 282-920.
Web: www.deutscheweine.de

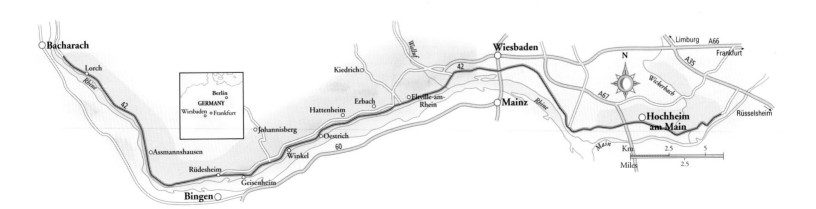

THE WACHAU

AND THE KREMSTAL

GILES MACDONOGH

The Wachau's enormous natural charm makes it a contender, with the Mosel and the Douro Valley, for the title of Europe's loveliest wine region. Between the thousand-year-old town of Krems and the great baroque monastery at Melk, huge cliffs of gneiss, granite, and mica schist rise up on either side of the serpentine River Danube. In the less perilous places the slopes have been seemingly hung with swags of vines. Picturesque villages and small towns punctuate the landscape: Loiben, Dürnstein, Mautern, and Weissenkirchen with their brightly colored houses festooned with pots of flowers; and through it all runs the great, reddy-brown Danube – it is only blue to those in love.

The Kremstal may be less ravishing, but it has its moments: the mother house of the Austrian Benedictine order, Stift Göttweig, is visible for miles around on top of its volcanic mound. It can be seen from the twin towns of Krems and Stein too, which certainly repay an afternoon's sight-seeing. Beauty has its drawbacks however, and tourists are a problem here. Cyclists clog up roads and pathways once the holidays begin and one gets the impression that many have been sent to the Wachau by their doctors: the sight of a flailing porpoise on a bicycle is rarely a pleasant one, and it makes driving, even walking, slow.

Climatically the Wachau and the Kremstal are more diverse than they initially seem; near Krems the weather is 'Pannonian': blown in from the hot Hungarian plains. (Pannonia was a Roman Danube province, situated mostly in today's Hungary.) As you turn the corner beyond Dürnstein, the heat is dissipated. If the locals are to be believed, the weather is positively arctic by the time you reach Melk, some 18 miles (30 kilometers) upriver, and little wine is made here.

LEFT Framed in pre-harvest foliage, the town of Dürnstein as seen from Rossatz on the south bank of the Danube. Wines from this region are less distinguished than those from other parts of the Wachau.

The natural starting point for any tour of the region is Krems, with its concentration of restaurants and hotels. The town boasts a number of surviving Leserhöfe, wine press-houses formerly owned by the monasteries of Upper Austria and Bavaria, which were once supplied with wine from Krems and the Wachau. The best restaurant is the Kaiser von Österreich. The Steigenberger Avance is the only large hotel; Am Förthof, on the river in Stein, offers more individual service.

There are no vineyards near the center of town, but to the northeast is the large Sandgrube, which makes good veltliner wines of little pretension. Great Kremser wine comes from the steeper, rocky soils to the west, which nudge the Wachau, where the town's most famous vineyards, Kögl, Pfaffenberg, and Hund, are situated. The Undhof, owned by the Salomon family, once the uncrowned kings of Krems, has always been among the most reputable sources for these wines. In recent years, however, Ewald Walzer in Krems-Gneixendorf has produced astonishingly concentrated wines from grüner veltliner and riesling, two of the main grapes of the region.

Grüner veltliner accounts for over a third of Austrian wine, making dry whites which can taste of pineapples, lentils, or bay. At its greatest, it is reminiscent of white burgundy.

The rockier terrain stretches north up the Krems River towards Senftenberg. Here, two of the best growers around, Martin Nigl and Franz Proidl, work the dizzy slopes to produce some of the raciest rieslings in Austria.

Amarone comes exclusively from the same zone as Valpolicella. The perfectly ripe and healthy bunches of grapes destined for its production are picked by hand a few days before the rest of the harvest, and then left to dry for an average of 100 days in well-ventilated lofts. The most beautiful grape-drying lofts are those at Villa Novare. This splendid 18th-century palazzo is the head-quarters of the Bertani Wine Company,

renowned producers of Amarone. Another 'château' definitely worth visiting in this area is the Villa Serego Alighieri at Gargagnago, Valpolicella's oldest winemaking estate and the home of the last male descendant of the poet Dante. Its drying lofts are smaller and retain an attractive artisan ambience.

The concentration of the juice and the high sugar content which results from drying the grapes produces one of the world's most

majestically opulent dry red wines. Amarone is velvety textured and rounded, with good balancing acidity and soft tannins.

Its traditional partners are beef braised in the wine, venison, and mature cheeses. However, its cooked cherry fruit and subtle hints of raisins and spices – a direct result of the semi-dried grapes used in its production – allow Amarone to be paired with the sweet and sour flavors of Chinese, Latin American and Indian cuisine. Some Amarone fans choose to serve it as a course in itself before dessert. In the zone, it is most often sipped outside of mealtimes, with good conversation and good friends.

Recioto della Valpolicella, a sweet red wine from semi-dried corvina, rondinella, and molinara grapes, is also made here (as it has been since Roman times). It is usually served with dry pastries or plain sponge cake.

East of Verona the gentle landscape changes to a dramatic, sweeping range of hills and abrupt gorges that are the result of prehistoric volcanic eruptions. Here the Valpolicella zone gives way to, and at points overlaps with, the Soave zone. The tiny

BELOW At Gargagnago in the Valpolicella Classico zone, grapes destined for Amarone are harvested by hand from canopy-trained vines.

BELOW RIGHT Vineyards near Affi, a small town in the Bardolino zone, lying at the mouth of the Adige Valley, close to the entrance to the Brenner Pass.

historic center of this zone is limited to a few hillsides around the medieval town of Soave and the hamlet of Monteforte d'Alpone. A winding cobblestone path off one of Soave's narrow streets brings you to the town's impressive castle. From here, on clear days, it is possible to see all the vineyards of the zone.

When yields are kept low and care is taken, Soave can be zesty and dry, with a bright, pale straw color. The main grape variety is garganega, with the possible addition of small amounts of trebbiano di Soave or chardonnay. The simple, floral style of basic Soave makes a fine aperitif and goes well with antipasti. More substantial Soaves are excellent with fish or vegetable-based rice and pasta dishes. Perhaps the ideal pairing for a fine well-structured, single-vineyard Soave is grilled freshwater fish, seasoned with rosemary and basted with the wine itself.

The Soave zone has the distinction of having the Veneto's first DOCG wine, Recioto di Soave, a sweet white made from semi-dried garganega grapes. Good Recioto is a gem that

has poise and balance, with luscious perfumes of green tea and honey. Particularly opulent versions go well with blue cheese or the crumbly local cake called *sbrisolona*.

Up in the mountains, just a few miles beyond the Soave zone, is the tiny town of Bolca, home to one of the world's most impressive fossil museums. On display are prehistoric fossilized grape leaves, palm trees and sharks, all of which were found locally and testify to the area's marine origins and its very long viticultural heritage.

Why not end each day's outing at a different café in one of Verona's many piazzas? One evening, enjoy a cool Soave at a table in Piazza Bra, across from the Roman amphitheater (one of the largest in the world); the next, nurse a warming Amarone in Piazza delle Erbe, which served as the city's forum in Roman times. The cafés in Piazza dei Signori, with its combination of Roman remains, medieval rigor and Renaissance elegance, offer a magical setting in which to sip a good Recioto.

VENETO

MAIN GRAPES

Red: Corvina, rondinella, molinara, corvinone, merlot, cabernet sauvignon and cabernet franc.
White: Garganega, trebbiano di Soave, prosecco.

LEADING WINES (DOC/DOCG zones):

Bardolino, Valpolicella, Amarone della Valpolicella, Recioto della Valpolicella, Soave, Recioto di Soave, Prosecco di Conegliano-Valdobbiadene, Breganza, Colli Berici, Colli Euganei.

MAIN PRODUCERS

(Phone in advance to make an appointment.)
Valpolicella/Amarone: Allegini, Bertani, Brolo di Musella, Brunelli, Serego Alighieri, Quintarelli, Dal Forno, Speri, Tommasi, Masi, Viviani, Tenuta Sant'Antonio, Trabucchi, Corte Sant'Alda.
Bardolino: Le Fraghe, Corte Gardoni, Zeni, Lamberti, Guerrieri-Rizzardi, Le Tende, Costadoro, Villabella, Cavalchina, Bolla, Monte del Frà, Zenato.
Soave and Recioto di Soave:
Anselmi, Ca'Rugate, Cantina del Castello, Coffele, La Cappuccina, Gini, Inama, Pieropan, Portinari, Pra, Suavia, Tenuta Casarsa, Terre dei Monti, Vicentini, Zenato.

MAIN TOWNS Verona, Soave, Bardolino.

DAYS Four.

BEST TIME TO GO April to November.

May: *Mangnalunga,* a gastronomic walk through Valpolicella; May/June: medieval fair in Soave; July/Aug: lake tours from Bardolino; August: opera at the Arena in Verona; October/November: Grape Festival and Novello Wine Festival in Bardolino, or visit the drying lofts.

SUMMARY Based in Verona, with visits to the

vineyards of Valpolicella and Amarone, Soave and Bardolino. Additional day trips may be made to Venice, Padua and Vicenza, all of which are less than two hours away.

LEFT Luscious garganega grapes being dried in the traditional manner for Recioto di Soave.
CENTER The Arena, Verona's first-century Roman amphitheater, hosts a summer season of open-air operas and regular classical concerts.
RIGHT Trattorias like this one in Negrar serve good value traditional specialties to locals and tourists alike.

SOURCES OF INFORMATION

• *Consorzio per la Tutela dei Vini DOC Soave e Recioto di Soave* (Soave Consortium)
via XXV Aprile 8, 37038 Soave, Italy.
Tel: +39 (45) 768-1578
Fax: +39 (45) 619-0306.
Email: consorzio@ilsoave.com
Web: www.ilsoave.com
• Verona Tourist Office
Email: info@tourism.verona.it
Web: www.tourism.verona.it

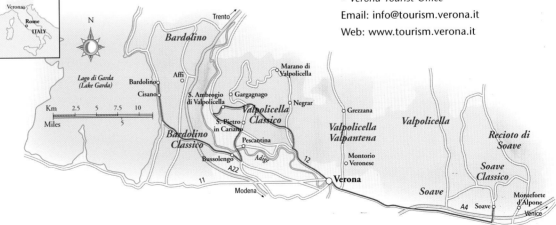

RIOJA AND NAVARRA

JOHN RADFORD

Midday in the Plaza de la Paz in Haro, Rioja: old ladies are peeling bright red peppers and chopping chorizo (spicy sausage) for lunch while their grandchildren skateboard across the cobbles around the bandstand. Small cars hoot and radiate heat-haze as they queue through the archway beside the town hall, where the flags of Spain and La Rioja hang lazily in the sun against the bleached sandstone walls. This small town is the spiritual home of Rioja wine.

That morning you could have come down from Bilbao, making the climb up the north side of the Cantabrian mountains, through the crags and pine forests in the greenest part of Spain. Then, at the summit, the descent begins into warmer air and drier landscape, with the valley of the river Ebro in the distance, and the first vineyards. If it's just before harvest-time they'll be heavy with glossy black grapes: this is the southern part of the Basque country, and they like their tempranillo ripe, fresh, and juicy.

At about two o'clock you could have lunch at Terete, on the other side of Haro town hall. It's a very simple local place that serves some of the best chorizo and *cordero asado* (roast lamb) in Spain. It also has an impressive list of old Rioja wines and, unusually, its own-label (or house) Reserva and Gran Reserva wines are among the best, and the cheapest, on the list. Situated elsewhere in the town, some of the most famous bodegas (wineries) welcome visitors, among them CVNE (*Compañía Vinícola del Norte de España*), Muga and La Rioja Alta.

The wine takes its name from the unremarkable Río Oja which runs into the slightly bigger Río Tirón which then runs through Haro to join the mighty Ebro to the north. Wine has been made here since Roman times, and the name was first recorded in the 11th century, but the big change came in the 1850s when a number of local pioneers (most notably the companies we now know as Marqués de Murrieta and de Riscal) imported 'new' winemaking technology from

LEFT Bottles of Rioja maturing at Castillo de Monjardín. Strict regulations determine the minimum length of time the oak-aged wine must mature in bottles or tanks before it can be released.

ABOVE LEFT Vineyards in the foothills of the Sierra de Cantabria, Rioja Alavesa, are wetter and cooler and produce some of the region's best grapes.

ABOVE CENTER Bodegas Marqués de Murrieta at Ygay, near Logorono. The young Count Vicente Cebrian took over the estate in the mid-1990s after the death of his father.

ABOVE RIGHT Bodegas López de Heredia in Haro is one of the most traditional of all the bodegas in Rioja, with vast cellars of fabulous old wines.

Bordeaux and set about improving the local production. When France's vineyards were ravaged by the phylloxera plague, the wine of Rioja found a ready export market across the Pyrenees, and it has remained France's favorite non-French wine ever since.

Heading eastwards from Haro, the river Ebro divides the Rioja Alavesa in the north, with its higher, cooler vineyards, from the Rioja Alta on the south bank. The winding road to Laguardia reveals more famous names between the rolling plains of wheat and vines: in Cenicero there's Unión Vitivinícola (better known as Marqués de Cáceres) and Elciego, the home of one of the two original pioneers, Marqués de Riscal.

Laguardia itself is a beautifully preserved fortified hill-town, with its ancient walls and narrow streets, red peppers drying on balconies in the summer and a magnificent view over the valley below. Bodegas Palacio is here and there's a magnificent small hotel/restaurant, Castillo El Collado, within the walls of the town.

Laserna, between Laguardia and Logroño, has Contino, one of the most beguiling estates. The beautifully preserved 16th-century farmhouse set in its own vineyards produces one of the region's finest wines.

Logroño, the business capital of La Rioja, is a big, bustling city with wide boulevards and a central square, the *Espolón*, from which you can visit the cathedral, the tourist office, or just dream the afternoon away in the shade of the plane trees. Meat-eaters agree that the best restaurant in town is probably Mesón Egües, just off the Vitoria road, west of the city center. Logroño is home to some famous-name bodegas such as Olarra, Ijalba and Campo Viejo. Just outside town on the Zaragoza road is the other great pioneer of modern Rioja wine, Marqués de Murrieta.

Southwest lies the Rioja Baja, which is hotter, lower and sandier, and where the rich, plump garnacha grape is king. From here, strike northeast into neighboring Navarra on the Pamplona road, bidding Rioja goodbye as you pass Ondarre in the village of Viana.

Navarra's approach to wine embraces almost every aspect of new technology. A prime example is the Castillo de Monjardín at Villamayor de Monjardín. The beautiful old sandstone buildings, surrounded by vineyards, include a restaurant and tasting rooms, with a sparkling modern winery built on. The wines are very much new-wave Navarra and set the tone for much of what is happening in the region.

The next stopping-place is Ayegui, on the Camino de Santiago – the ancient pilgrim route from Germany and France to Santiago de Compostela in the northwest of Spain. To this day, pilgrims traveling on foot (or on a donkey) can claim free accommodation, food, and wine from monasteries and lodging houses en route. The Camino passes along the perimeter wall of Bodegas Irache, which provides a drinking fountain for passers-by in a small courtyard inside the wall. One tap dispenses water, the other wine and, to pilgrims, both are free.

Head southeast, to Tafalla and thence to Olite, the unspoilt ancient capital of Navarra, with its 15th-century castle and cathedral. The magnificent former residence of the kings of Navarra is now a parador (hotel), and the medieval city walls are still substantially intact. One of the most important bodegas

here is Ochoa, but it is only open by appointment. If you want to see some of the most cutting-edge wine research being carried out in Spain, it's possible, also by appointment, to visit EVENA, the Navarra wine research establishment, which is housed in an old distillery building just north of the town.

Heading south beyond Tudela, the small towns of Murchante and Cascante are home to several major bodegas. Principe de Viana in Murchante is a modern, high-production company turning out good-quality middle-market wines at reasonable prices.

In neighboring Cascante, opposite the bullring, is Guelbenzu, a family-owned business which, after years in the doldrums, recovered in the early 1990s and now produces some of Navarra's finest wines. The

LEFT Free wine and water are available at the Pilgrims' Fountain at Bodegas Irache, on the ancient road to Santiago de Compostela.

BOTTOM LEFT Commercial management at Guelbenzu is overseen by Ricardo Guelbenzu, one of the seven sons of 92-year-old patriarch Julio.

lovely old house includes the small winery where the wines are made, and can be visited by appointment.

Take a detour northwest to Cintruénigo and the house of Chivite, which has the accolade of being the oldest in Navarra, having been in business since 1647. Indeed, for many years the vast majority of wine in the export market was from Chivite and the company is still respected as one of the pioneers of modern Navarra wine.

Now it's time to head north to Pamplona (the A15 autopista is quickest), although there's a side-visit worth exploring if you have the time, to Ujué, a tiny hill-village in the middle of nowhere (take the Tafalla exit and head east). The church is beautiful, the views spectacular, and the Mesón Las Torres will serve you lamb chops or *migas*, a local dish of hot breadcrumbs, chopped ham, peppers, and spices, both cooked over an open fire and served with unlabeled bottles of red house Navarra.

And then it's on to Pamplona, the city of Ernest Hemingway, where, between 6 and 14 July, if you're up for it, you can run with the bulls in the narrow city streets during the festival of San Fermín. Or you may prefer to sit in the Plaza del Castillo with an early-evening apéritif and decide which of the city's excellent restaurants shall earn your patronage tonight. Josetxo on the Plaza Principe de Viana, and Rodero, behind the bullring, are generally adjudged the best, but La Chistera, on the Calle St Nicolas, is very good and about half the price. Depending on the wine you choose, of course …

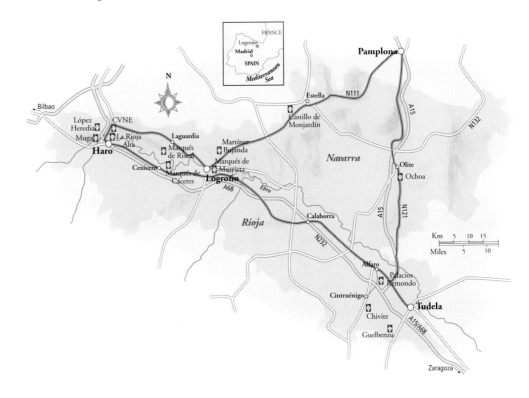

FAR LEFT Red peppers, such as these drying on a balcony in Laguardia, are used in dishes like *caldereta de cordero*, a lamb stew with peppers and onions.
LEFT Only a few bodegas continue to make their own barrels, but the odd perfectionist, such as here at Guelbenzu, still insists on it.

SUMMARY Haro – Laguardia – Laserna – Logroño – Estella – Olite – Tudela – Cintruénigo – Pamplona.

SOURCES OF INFORMATION

Both regions publish a booklet on visiting bodegas. Telephone ahead before all visits to ensure that the bodegas are able to receive you.
• **Rioja:** *CRDOCa Rioja, Estambrera 52, 26006 Logroño.*
Tel: +34 (941) 500-400
Fax: +34 (941) 500-672.
E-mail: info@riojawine.com
Web: www.riojawine.com.
• **Navarra:** *CRDO Navarra, Rua Romana s/n, 31390 Olite.*
Tel: +34 (948) 741-812
Fax: +34 (948) 741-776.

MAIN GRAPES

Red: Tempranillo, garnacha (both regions), cabernet sauvignon (Navarra only).
White: Chardonnay (Navarra).

LEADING WINES DOCa Rioja; DO Navarra.

MAIN PRODUCERS

Rioja: Age; Artadi; Barón de Ley; Berberana; Campo Viejo; Contino; CVNE; Faustino; LAN; López de Heredia; Marqués de Cáceres; Marqués de Griñón; Marqués de Murrieta; Marqués de Riscal; Martínez Bujanda; Muga; Olarra; Palacio; Palacios Remondo; Remelluri; La Rioja Alta.
Navarra: Castillo de Monjardín; Chivite; Guelbenzu; Gurpegui; Irache; Ochoa; Principe de Viana; Señorío de Sarría.

MAIN TOWNS

Rioja: Haro; Laguardia; Logroño.
Navarra: Olite; Pamplona.

ACCESS
Bilbao airport to Logroño – 92 miles (147km), Bilbao seaport to Logroño – 97 miles (156km); Madrid to Logroño – 198 miles (319km).

DAYS One week.

BEST TIME TO GO Most bodegas are open all year round, although many close for August. Spring and fall are the most comfortable times for touring.

JEREZ
THE SHERRY COUNTRY

JOHN RADFORD

Imagine a place where the streets are lined with trees laden with bitter Seville oranges in season, where the bodegas are set about with airy pathways sheltered by overhanging vines against the fierce summer sun, where the houses have cool, internal patios in the Moorish style, and where they care passionately about three things – horses, bulls and wine. You're imagining the sherry country, deep in the heart of Andalucía in southwest Spain.

They've been making wine here for about 2500 years and have developed a style that is unique in the world. Sherry as we know it today has evolved from a naturally strong and sweet wine made by immigrants from Greece in the fifth century BC. It was the wine's strength that made it 'tradable' (in other words, it traveled well enough to be salable at its destination), and when the Moors introduced distillation and the wine was fortified with spirit, it became even more valuable. The final element in sherry's success was the solera system in which new wine is blended with older wine over a period of years, providing wonderful consistency and quality. In Shakespeare's time, sherris-sack, as it was then called, was the finest wine in the world.

Sherry then was what we know today as oloroso – old, dry, fragrant and nutty – and these wines are still made, although the main market for oloroso today is in sweetened versions sold as cream sherry. In the 1850s the world saw the first fino sherry, which grows a covering of yeast in the barrel that separates the wine from the air and gives it a fresh, yeasty, nutty character. These are the wines, made entirely from the palomino grape, that have captured the imagination of a new generation of wine-lovers; pale in color, bone-dry on the palate and perfect with the tapas and seafood that are such an integral part of Andaluz cookery.

LEFT A vine-arbored road provides welcome shade between the bodegas of González Byass, the world's largest producer of sherry, still run today by the same family that founded the house in 1835. The company's top-selling fino brand, Tio Pepe, has been in existence since 1849.

The wines are made in and around a 'golden triangle' formed by the main sherry towns, Jerez de la Frontera, Puerto de Santa María and Sanlúcar de Barrameda. Jerez is the furthest inland, while Puerto is on the inshore side of Cádiz harbour, and Sanlúcar is on the estuary of the river Guadalquívir. The

two coastal towns make the freshest and most delicate finos, and those from Sanlúcar are known as manzanilla.

But we must begin in Jerez. The town is small enough to get around on foot and by taxi and the one-way system is complex enough to make this the preferred option. The main road in from the airport is the Avenida Alcalde Alvaro Domecq and, if you're fortunate enough to be in Jerez in the third week in May, at the time of the *Feria del Caballo* (horse fair – although that terse name hardly describes the reality), you'll see the Parque González Hontoria decked with flags and lights and full of people. Many will be wearing traditional costume, dancing the flamenco, admiring the magnificent horses and carriages which promenade throughout

the afternoon, and drinking sherry and eating tapas at the hundreds of little *casetes*, or pavilions, that are erected for the week by almost every business in the town. The other major festival in Jerez, the *Fiesta de la Vendimia*, celebrating the grape harvest, is held during the last week of September.

Jerez is one of the most wonderful places to eat, with even the smallest restaurants offering excellent fresh seafood, *jabugo* ham (from the semi-wild, free-range black pigs of neighboring Huelva) and various other local specialties. One of the best restaurants is La Mesa Redonda, whose *solomillo de iberico al oloroso* (fillet of *jabugo* in oloroso sauce) is legendary, and you'll find that a good deal of sherry, even the heavier dry oloroso, is drunk quite naturally with food.

BELOW LEFT The Sandeman Don logo, seen here on the facade of one of the bodegas, is one of the most famous in the wine trade.

BELOW RIGHT *Arrumbadores* (cellarmen) roll a barrel of sherry through Osborne's La Palma bodega in Puerto de Santa María.

OPPOSITE Harvesting palomino grapes at González Byass. The white *albariza* (a local term for the chalky limestone soil) gives sherry its character.

The Avenida Alcalde Alvaro Domecq reaches the town center at the Plaza de Mamelón. Nearby are the bodegas (cellars) of Sandeman, Wisdom and Warter, Garvey, Valdespino, and Williams & Humbert. Tours are conducted daily at Sandeman (lovely old bodegas dating to the 19th century) and Williams & Humbert (some fabulous vintage wines). Heading south and east of the town center you'll find Emilio Lustau (visits by appointment), next door to John Harvey and Diez-Merito (which has regular tours).

Two of the most famous names are quite close together, west of the *Alcázar* (castle) and to the south of the town center. Domecq's offices have a central atrium, with a small

museum devoted to the family's history – look out for the famous moped upon which the late head of the family, José-Ignacio Domecq, together with his dog Paco in a dog-basket, rode to work every day.

The other famous name is González Byass and, if you only get the chance to see one bodega in Jerez, this should be it. It occupies what was formerly an old corner of the city. Many years ago, frustrated by increasing traffic volumes, the company bought the neighboring streets from the city council and walled them off. You can still see the street names and the cobbles, and in summer there's a canopy of vines overhead. One of the bodegas, La Concha, was designed

by Gustave Eiffel, of tower (and Statue of Liberty) fame, and the central courtyard has its own museum devoted to the González family, as well as the famous Apóstoles. These are 12 large barrels named after the disciples, dominated by an even bigger cask in the center, known as El Cristo.

Head down the N-IV towards Puerto de Santa María, to the sparkling new bodegas of the Marqués del Real Tesoro. The company's origins date to 1860, but it lay dormant for many years before being bought in 1990 by the Estévez family. Since then no expense has been spared. There are regular tours here, too.

Puerto de Santa María has developed as a tourist resort, with a stunning new marina

specializes in local seafood, pulled from the harbor each day and cooked in the traditional Andaluz manner.

From Puerto you can head along the coast through Rota and Chipiona or strike out across country to Sanlúcar de Barrameda. The country route passes through some of the region's best vineyards, notably Miraflores, where some of the very best grapes for manzanilla grow.

In Sanlúcar they make the lightest and most delicate of wines; cooled by the sea breezes, it matures very crisp, light and bone-dry in the bodegas and much of it is drunk locally as a dry white wine in the seafood restaurants which range across the seafront. Probably the best of these is Casa Bigote, a place where the fish comes straight from the beach and the entrance to the restaurant is through the kitchen, so you can see it being cooked. Famous names in Sanlúcar include Barbadillo and Vinícola Hidalgo, both of whom accept visitors by appointment. Javier Hidalgo is a great conservationist, and a vigorous and generous supporter of the Coto de Doñana, the largest and most unspoilt wetland area in Europe, which is just across the river to the north.

The best thing about the sherry country, however, is the sheer enjoyment the local people derive from living, working, eating, and drinking in some of Spain's most delightful small cities, with the coast never more than a few miles away and one of the world's oldest fine wines being ever rediscovered by a new generation of sherry-lovers. One of the finest pleasures of the civilized world is to sit outside a bar, under an orange tree on a spring evening, with a range of tapas and a selection of sherry wines experimenting with tastes and flavors.

and views across the harbor to the city of Cádiz. In wine terms, it is most famous for its finos, although all styles of wine are made here. It is the home of Luís Caballero (visits by appointment), the company which now owns Emilio Lustau. Probably the best-known bodega is Osborne (also famous for its brandy), whose main building is modern, but in the classic Andaluz style. The wines are splendid, but visits are by appointment only.

Puerto has one of the best restaurants in the sherry country, El Faro de Puerto, which

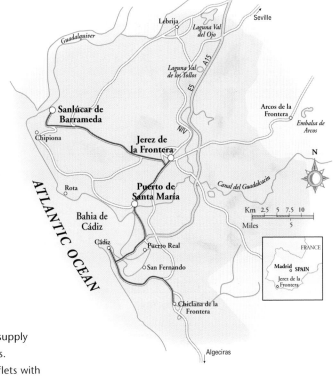

ABOVE Manuel Arcila (left) and Manuel (Manolo) Grimaldi of Emilio Lustau taste fino sherry from the cask. A *venencia* is being used to pour the wine.

ABOVE RIGHT The Valdespino and Viña la Merced properties near Jerez de la Frontera. The best vineyards are planted in the chalk soil whilst lesser soils are often used for sunflowers.

MAIN GRAPES

White: Palomino, pedro ximénez, moscatel.

LEADING WINES
Jerez/Xérès/Sherry, Manzanilla de Sanlúcar de Barrameda.

MAIN PRODUCERS

Jerez: Barbadillo, Croft, Domecq, González Byass, Harvey, Lustau, Marqués del Real Tesoro, Sandeman, Williams & Humbert.
Puerto de Santa Maria: Osborne.
Sanlúcar deBarrameda: Vinícola Hidalgo.

MAIN TOWNS
Jerez de la Frontera, Puerto de Santa María, Sanlúcar de Barrameda.

AIRPORTS
Jerez, Seville.

DAYS
One week.

BEST TIME TO GO
Spring and fall are the most comfortable for touring, and also the time of the most exciting festivals.

SUMMARY
Jerez – Puerto de Santa María – Sanlúcar de Barrameda.

SOURCES OF INFORMATION

• *Oficina Municipal de Turismo* (Jerez Tourist Office) Larga 39, 11403 Jerez de la Frontera.
Tel: +34 (956) 331-150,
Fax: +34 (956) 331-731.
• *CRDO Jerez/Xérès/Sherry y Manzanilla de Sanlúcar*
Avenida Alvaro Domecq 2,
11405 Jerez de la Frontera.
Tel: +34 (956) 332-050,
Fax: +34 (956) 338-908.
E-mail: vinjerez@sherry.org
Web: www.sherry.org
The Consejo Regulador (CRDO) can supply information about individual bodegas. The Jerez Tourist Office publishes leaflets with details on which bodegas operate regular tours. Telephone ahead to ensure that the bodegas are able to receive you.

DOURO VALLEY

JIM BUDD

The vineyards of the Douro are some of the most spectacular, beautiful and isolated in the world and, until very recently, this was the most difficult wine region in Western Europe to visit. In many parts of the upper Douro you feel that you have reached the world's end. Fortunately though, the valley is now being opened up to wine visitors.

Of course it has long been easy to visit Oporto (Porto) and the port lodges in Vila Nova de Gaia on the south bank of the river, where the wine is matured, but the vineyards of the Douro, especially those in the upper Douro close to the Spanish border, have always been fairly inaccessible. Until the fast road was built from Oporto to Vila Real, north of Pinhão, it took three or four hours to drive up to Pinhão in the center of the port vineyards. Unfortunately, having got there, it was almost impossible to find anywhere to stay, unless you were lucky enough to be accommodated at one of the *quintas* (estates) of the port producers.

This situation is now changing, with a few hotels opening along with bed and breakfast and self-catering places, many of which are at small port *quintas*. It is still essential, however, to book accommodation before you leave as, unlike other European wine regions, it is often impossible to find rooms as you go. You should also book appointments with *quintas* in the Douro. Do take care when driving, especially when you have been tasting. Many of the roads are very narrow with precipitous drops, and there is no margin for error. Visiting the Douro remains an adventure – but what an adventure!

Port owes its success to the long love-hate relationship between England and France and the 600-year alliance between Portugal and England. In the latter part of the 17th century, imports of French wine into Britain were banned and merchants turned to Portugal. Unfortunately Portuguese wine was of such poor quality that brandy had to be added to help it travel and to

LEFT View across the Douro from Vila Nova de Gaia to Oporto. Traditional *barcos rabelos* are now largely for show; before the upper Douro was dammed they were used to ship port from the *quintas* high up the valley.

LEFT AND ABOVE Many of the port lodges in Vila Nova de Gaia have a visitor's center and tasting room, including Ferreira (left) and Graham's (above). Ferreira, one of the leading port companies, was established in 1715; this section of the building used to be a monastery.

OPPOSITE The recently established Vintage House Hotel at Pinhão is a sign that the upper Douro is at last being opened up for visitors. Pinhão makes an excellent base from which to explore the area.

make it taste more palatable. Originally the brandy spirit was added after fermentation was complete, but gradually people started using spirit to stop the fermentation, leaving the wines sweet. Thus port was born. Today grape spirit (*aguardente*) at 77 percent is added once the alcohol reaches about eight percent, to bring port up to 20 percent alcohol. Then the wine is matured for a varying length of time, depending on the desired style of the port being made.

All good quality ports are aged in wood. The most commonly sized barrel is 145 gallons (550 liters) and is called a pipe (the standard volume of measurement in the port trade).

There are two main types of quality port: vintage and tawny. A vintage port is declared only in good years and spends two years in wood before being bottled when its color is still a deep crimson plum. Tawnies, on the other hand, spend a long time in wood

before being bottled and so gradually lose their fruit colour. Instead they develop shades of brown and walnut – hence their name. Most companies offer a range of tawnies, usually 10, 20, 30, and 40 years old.

Any journey to the Douro must include a few days in Oporto and Vila Nova de Gaia. The logical order would be to visit the vineyards in the Douro and then return to Oporto to visit the lodges in Vila Nova de Gaia. Built on the steep slopes rising up from the Douro, and with a series of spectacular bridges over the river, Oporto is an atmospheric city, especially at night, when its bars and restaurants come alive along the waterfront. A double-decked steel bridge built by French engineer Ferdinand De Lesseps, of Suez Canal fame, is the central attraction and carries two roads and a railway.

Many of the port lodges are open to visitors. They start on the waterfront at Vila

Nova de Gaia and stretch up the steep slopes behind, served by very narrow roads which, although traffic-choked, add to the old-world atmosphere. Calém and Sandeman are among the best set up for visitors.

In the past, port was shipped down the Douro to Oporto in *barcos rabelos*, small flat-bottomed boats with a single sail. The journey was often dangerous yet, despite the arrival of the railway in the 1880s, the boats were used until the mid-1960s when the river was dammed. Now they are kept for the shippers' annual race in Oporto on 24 June.

Before leaving Oporto it is worth visiting the Bolhão market off the Sa de Bandeira in the old part of the city. Invariably there are stalls with mounds of thinly sliced green cabbage, ready for *caldo verde*, the cabbage soup that starts so many Portuguese meals.

Ideally the journey up the Douro starts at the imposing and ornate station in Oporto.

Despite the beautiful blue and white tiles (*azulejos*) in the entrance hall, there is a sense of glories past, as the main line now bypasses the center of the town. Departing trains plunge into a tunnel at the end of the platform, adding to the sense of mystery and expectation. This is one of the great train journeys of the world, especially if you remember to sit on the right-hand side for the trip up the valley. During the first hour, as you clear the outskirts of Oporto and travel past fields, vineyards and villages in a gently rolling landscape, there is no hint of what is to come. It is not until the train makes the long descent down to the river that the journey becomes beautiful for, from this point, the railway hugs the river. Only by taking the train is it possible to see certain parts of the valley, as the road has to go up over the hills, especially in the upper Douro.

An alternative to taking the train is to drive. There are two routes: the slower, but picturesque, N108 up the Douro, part of which is untarred; or, for those more pressed for time, the fast modern road that runs north of the Douro to Amarante, from where you can either cut down by Mesão Frio to the river or head for Vila Real and then down to Pinhão. Quinta do Portal at Celeirós do Douro can be visited on the way. A cruise up the Douro is also possible.

After two hours the train reaches Regua, the largest town on the river after Oporto, which has been spoilt by insensitive development. Regua is in the Baixo Corgo, the smallest and most westerly of the three port-producing areas. The nearby Quinta da Casa Amarela at Riobom-Cambres is a small port producer worth a visit. Quinta Sol, part of the Symington group, is also open to visitors.

Pinhão is a further 45 minutes upstream on a bend of the Douro. This small town, more an overgrown village, is the center of Cima Corgo, with a number of important *quintas* close to it and in the surrounding hillsides. Since the recent opening of the Vintage House hotel by the Taylor's Group, Pinhão has become the most sensible base for visiting the Douro vineyards.

A few steps from the railway station in Pinhão is Quinta do Bomfim, also part of the Symington group. Above the town is Quinta do Noval, one of the showcase estates of the region, now owned by AXA Millésimes. This historic estate has been renovated, in particular the famous terraces. Noval is one of the few companies to age its wines up in the Douro rather than at Vila Nova de Gaia.

In nearby Vale de Mendiz is the Museo dos Lagares, set up by Sandeman. *Lagares* are the traditional granite tanks where port is fermented and the grapes are trodden by the feet of teams of workers, often accompanied by music and singing. Also worth visiting is Fonseca's Quinta do Panascal on the Rio Távora, on the south side of the Douro.

An increasing amount of still red wine is now being made in the Douro. First made in the 1950s, Ferreira's Barca Velha was the precursor. Among the recent successes is Quinta do Crasto near the hamlet of Ferrão.

Beyond Pinhão the already spectacular scenery increases in grandeur, becoming wilder and more sparsely populated. There are no roads close to the river, only the railway, which clings grimly to the precipitous slopes, making this a breathtaking ride. The train continues to Tua and on to Ferradoza, just past the dam at Valeira. This is the Douro Superior. The next stop is the private station at Taylor's top *quinta*, de Vargellas, which, sadly, is not open to the public. The train continues past Vesúvio until it reaches its terminus at Pocinho. It used to go on to the Spanish border but no longer does. In any case, this is beyond the port production zone.

In late 2001 the upper Douro was proclaimed by UNESCO as a World Heritage Site.

BELOW Many *quintas*, such as Bomfim, retain the step-like terraces excavated in the 19th century, although ramps are increasingly replacing them.

MAIN GRAPES

Red: Tinta amarela, tinta barroca, tinta roriz, tinta cão, touriga francesca, touriga naçional.

LEADING WINES

Ports: Vintage, Tawny Port (10, 20, 30, 40 Year Old), Colheitas, Crusted Port, Late Bottle Vintage.
Douro reds: Barca Velha, Quinta do Crasto, Quinta do Portal.

MAIN PRODUCERS

Cálem, Churchill, Cockburn, Dow, Ferreira, Fonseca, Graham, Quinta do Noval, Taylor's, Sandeman, Quinta do Vesúvio, Warre.

SOME QUINTAS TO VISIT (Appointments are usually essential.) Quinta do Bomfin, Quinta da Casa Amarela, Quinta dos Lagares, Quinta do Noval, Quinta do Panascal, Quinta do Portal, Quinta Sol.

Some port lodges to visit: Cálem, Ferreira, Graham, Sandeman (includes a museum).

MAIN TOWN AND AIRPORT Oporto.

DAYS Three to four.

BEST TIME TO GO April to November, but avoid the height of the summer.

SUMMARY Oporto – Pinhão.

SOURCES OF INFORMATION

• *Gabinete da Rota do Vinho do Porto* (Port Wine Route), Rua dos Camilos 90, 5050 Peso da Régua. Tel: +51 (351) 254-320-145.
• *Institute do Vinho do Porto* (Port Wine Institute) Rua Ferreira Borges, 4050 Porto.
Tel: +51 (351) 222-071-600.
Web: www.ivp.pt

LEFT Ancient and modern combine at Quinta do Bomfim in Pinhão, where shiny stainless steel tanks stand beside traditional cement vats.

CENTRE The traditional blue and white tiles, *azulejos*, are a feature of a number of railway stations on the line up the Douro.

RIGHT Workers picking grapes at Taylor's Quinta da Vargellas in the upper Douro are almost dwarfed by the steep terraces.

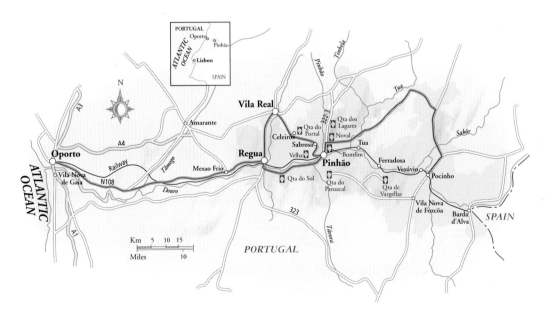

INTRODUCTION

THE NEW WORLD
FROM CHALLENGERS TO CHAMPIONS

JIM BUDD

There is a popular misconception that wines from outside Europe are something entirely new. This is reinforced by the shorthand terms Old and New World. Many 'new' wine-producing countries have a tradition of wine that goes back several hundred years. The first recorded vineyard in Argentina was in 1557. In South Africa, the first wine from the Cape was made in 1659. The first settlers in Australia planted grapes as soon as they arrived in the late 1780s. In contrast, much of the Médoc was salt marsh until Dutch engineers drained it during the 17th century, and Château Lafite-Rothschild was probably not planted until the latter third of that century.

It is certainly true that since the mid-1960s there have been very big changes in California, as well as over the past 15 years or so in countries like Australia, Chile, and New Zealand, which have altered the face of the traditional wine world. It was not until 1973, for instance, that the first sauvignon blanc vines were planted in the Marlborough district, where they have flourished, becoming New Zealand's great success story.

Many New World producers are characterized by their open-mindedness and dynamism. Unlike their counterparts in Europe, they are less hidebound by tradition and regulations. Due to the practice of naming wines by the grape variety used, the New World has helped to demystify wine and to create new wine enthusiasts. Varietal wine names are easy to pronounce and they avoid a daunting plethora of foreign names that require an encyclopedic knowledge of geography and a detailed recall of producers. New World growers can also plant whatever varieties they like wherever they wish. This is not to say that where the vines are planted is not just as important in the New World as it is in the Old. Any gardener with more than a window box to look after knows that plants should be put where the micro-climate and soil are best suited to them. Vines are no different: flat, fertile land is ideal for vegetables, while vines give their best fruit in thin, well drained soils.

Until the 1960s Australia concentrated on fortified wines before turning to table wines, initially with the accent on white varieties before concentrating on reds as wine drinkers' preferences changed. South Africa followed a similar pattern, moving from semi-sweet whites and heavy overblown reds to the classic varietal wines preferred by discerning drinkers today. All over, the move towards quality wine consumption went hand-in-hand with the opening of wineries to the public. Most New World wineries are set up to welcome visitors, with tasting rooms, cellar tours and even shops selling their own wines and other items such as clothing, home-grown produce and luxury foods. Many also have a restaurant or picnic area. Some of the best restaurants in Australia, California, and South Africa are attached to wineries, with the menu often tailor-made to show off the producer's wines.

In some areas wine tourism has become so successful that it is wise to avoid visiting the most popular wineries during peak holiday times. There are always plenty of lesser-known wineries a little off the beaten track where you will be welcomed with a smile by staff who are perhaps less harassed by the crowds. Of course, some wineries are not open to casual visitors at all. When output is limited and demand high, top-flight producers can sell their annual production many times over and there is no need to court passing traffic. Many of these 'icon' or cult wines are sold through mailing lists only, and the waiting lists are usually closed. California, Australia, and South Africa all have their share of highly desirable wines that are not readily available.

For the ordinary wine lover, wine tourism offers a way to try new styles and vintages, buy stocks at cellar prices, obtain information about how the wine was made and when it should be drunk, even to meet the winemaker in person. Even in Argentina and Chile, where wine tourism is in its infancy, all the finance going into wine projects ensures that it is likely to develop rapidly over the next decade.

LEFT French Farm, on the Banks Peninsula outside Christchurch, New Zealand, commemorates the early French settlers who were the very first wine growers here.

PREVIOUS PAGES The barrel cellar at Robert Mondavi's Opus One winery in Napa is testament to California's challenge to lead the New World in wine excellence.

NAPA VALLEY

STEPHEN BROOK

Napa Valley may not be the oldest of California's wine regions, but it is certainly the most prestigious. By the end of the 19th century it had acquired an international reputation for the quality of its red wines, and surviving wineries from this period, such as Far Niente, Niebaum-Coppola and Beringer, attest to the prosperity of the region.

All this renown was to be wiped out, first by phylloxera and then by Prohibition. Some of the wineries tottered through Prohibition and emerged at the other end in a tarnished and weary state from which it would take decades to recover. In the 1950s and 1960s about half the grapes from the valley's vineyards were vinified at a local cooperative under contract to Gallo, the largest winery in the world, which used it mostly for jug wines such as Hearty Burgundy.

Gradually, though, Napa Valley revived and when Robert Mondavi opened his Spanish colonial-style winery in Oakville in 1966, it was a new sign of confidence. Between 1960 and 1988 the number of wineries expanded from 20 to 204. In the 21st century Napa is still growing, with rich investors spending colossal sums for the last patches of land suitable for viticulture.

In the early days, a protracted battle was fought between those who were happy to see further commercial expansion of the valley and those who wished to preserve its beauty. Fortunately, the latter won in 1968, which means that, except along the highway that runs up the center of the valley, Napa is still worth visiting for its beautiful landscape alone. Indeed, not everyone comes to Napa for wine tourism: there are tranquil resort complexes, a plethora of great restaurants, and the thriving hot springs at Calistoga. If you wish, you can also forget about driving and take a leisurely ride on the Napa Wine Train as it chugs up the valley while attendants ply you with food and wine.

LEFT The Opus One winery at Oakville is a striking modern building designed by Scott Johnson of Los Angeles. The slope leading up to the winery entrance conceals a vast underground barrel cellar.

The producers have made it easy for the majority of visitors who come here to sample the wines. Most of the major wineries have well-organized tasting rooms and quite a few also have picnic facilities. Many visitors seek out a good delicatessen, such as the Oakville Grocery, buy some sandwiches or salads, stop at a favorite winery to taste and buy a bottle or two, and then settle down at a trestle table to enjoy an alfresco lunch in the usually balmy Napa sunshine. Many tasting rooms charge a fee, but this is invariably refunded if you make a purchase.

Napa is a relatively small narrow valley, some 30 miles (48 kilometers) or so from one end to the other, but it is surprisingly diverse. The southern end is prone to invasions of fog from the Pacific Ocean, which keeps the climate cool. Here, in the Carneros and Coombsville subregions, chardonnay, pinot noir and syrah are usually planted. Further north, around St Helena and Calistoga, where the maritime influence is less marked, the daytime temperatures are decidedly high, making this a perfect area for cabernet sauvignon and zinfandel. Twenty years ago it was easy to find varieties such as riesling, muscat and petite sirah, but they are now in decline, as demand is focused on the fashionable international varieties for which high prices can be obtained.

However, it has to be admitted that cabernet sauvignon excels better than any other variety in Napa, producing wines that can often rival the top growths of Bordeaux in price as well as quality. Napa cabernet has a wonderful richness, depth and fruitiness, and a hedonistic aspect that makes it more accessible than often austere Bordeaux. Merlot is increasingly sought after, and chardonnay is as popular as ever, although many parts of Napa are too warm for it.

Two roads traverse the valley from north to south: the busy Highway 29, and the more tranquil Silverado Trail from Napa to Calistoga. You should ascend the valley up Highway 29 and return on the Silverado Trail. Depending on your approach, you may find yourself on Route 12, which passes through the Carneros region, where many of California's top sparkling wines are made. Domaine Carneros and Artesa have fine tasting rooms and spacious terraces on which to enjoy the wines.

Drive up Highway 29 to Yountville, where you will see on the left the strange hangar-like winery of French-influenced Dominus (not open to visitors). Continue to Oakville, where the major landmark is the tower of the Mondavi winery, which offers one of the valley's most informative tours and tastings. Opposite is the architectural *tour de force* of Opus One, a joint venture between Robert Mondavi and Baron Philippe de Rothschild of the Bordeaux Mouton-Rothschild family.

As you approach Rutherford, the most prized sector of the valley, there

LEFT Frog's Leap Winery moved in 1994 to the handsome, century-old Red Barn in Rutherford, where John Williams makes delicious, stylish organically grown wines.

OPPOSITE The undulating hills and cooler climate of Carneros are ideal for chardonnay and pinot noir. Here, Mondavi's Huichica Hills vineyard overlooks San Pablo Bay.

are plenty of top-quality wineries to visit, among them Turnbull, Cakebread, Sequoia Grove, Frog's Leap and St Supéry, which has a fine visitors' center. At Niebaum-Coppola, the old Inglenook winery has been restored and is well worth a visit.

Continuing north to St Helena and Calistoga, wineries worth stopping at include Franciscan, Merryvale, Beringer and the architecturally controversial Clos Pegase; some visitors remark on its Minoan grandeur,

others liken it to a crematorium. Sterling is spectacular too, set up on a crag, but the wines are less exciting. In Calistoga itself don't miss Château Montelena (est. 1882), home of award winning chardonnay.

The Silverado Trail is just to the east of Highway 29 at Calistoga, so it's easy to find before heading south. Wineries to visit here include Cuvaison, Duckhorn, Sinskey, Pine Ridge, Stag's Leap, Miner, Clos du Val, and approaching Napa, the brand-new Darioush.

In Napa itself, generally a town of little interest, visit the stunning Copia, the American Center for Wine, Food, and the Arts.

This round trip would make for a fairly exhausting day or two, especially if combined with steady tastings. It's better to book into one of the many hotels in the valley and wander at a leisurely pace. The best budget choice is the Art Deco La Bonita Motel. Both St Helena and Calistoga are full of cozy (though not cheap) bed and breakfast places.

Many of the most fascinating wineries are not on the valley floor, but up in the mountains that flank the valley. To the east is Howell Mountain where, high above the fog line, some magnificent rugged cabernets are produced at Dun and La Jota, neither of which is open to the public. To the west are Mount Veeder, Spring Mountain, and Diamond Mountain, where some of the world's most visually spectacular vineyards are located. Sadly most of them, including

BELOW LEFT Sparkling wine producer Domaine Carneros is owned by the Taittinger family. The winery is a replica of their château in Champagne.
BELOW RIGHT Film director Francis Ford Coppola owns the former Inglenook estate, located around one of Napa's great 19th-century stone wineries.

Cain, Newton and Diamond Creek, are not open to the public, although Hess and Pride Mountain can be visited. Sometimes, an impassioned phone call may secure an appointment to visit a favorite estate not normally open to the casual visitor. It's almost certainly a waste of time though, to attempt to contact the cult wine producers such as Screaming Eagle or Bryant. With production limited to a few hundred cases at extravagant prices, and a long waiting list clamoring for just a few bottles each year, such wineries can afford to ignore even the most enthusiastic wine tourist.

Another reason to prolong your stay in the Napa valley is to sample its superb restaurants. The intriguingly named French Laundry in Yountville has been described as the best restaurant in America. It's certainly the most dazzling and inventive, but you must book at least a month in advance. Other outstanding and enjoyable restaurants include Catahoula in Calistoga, Celadon in Napa, Bouchon in Yountville, and in St Helena, Tra Vigne, Terra, Mustards Grill, and Pinot Blanc. Their wine lists often feature the hard-to-find bottles that excite American wine lovers and they are certainly worth trying – if price is no object.

Summer (June–August) inevitably, is not the best time to visit Napa Valley. The roads are choked, the restaurants and hotels booked up, and the tasting rooms are too crowded for enjoyment. But the valley can be visited with pleasure at just about any other time of the year. The harvest tends to be protracted, so even in September and October the wineries' hospitality is unabated.

NAPA VALLEY

ABOVE LEFT The Napa Valley wine train makes a sedate journey up the valley.
ABOVE RIGHT An outdoor buffet at Clos du Val winery, off the Silverado Trail.

MAIN GRAPES

Red: Cabernet sauvignon, merlot, zinfandel, pinot noir, syrah.
White: Chardonnay, sauvignon blanc, viognier.

LEADING APPELLATIONS (AVAS)

Carneros, Stag's Leap, Rutherford, Diamond Mountain, Spring Mountain, Mount Veeder, Howell Mountain, Oakville, Atlas Peak, Chiles Valley, St Helena, Yountville.

MAIN PRODUCERS

Beringer, Cakebread, Châteaux Montelena, Clos du Val, Duckhorn, Grgich Hills, Hess, Merryvale, Mondavi, Niebaum-Coppola, Opus One, Pride Mountain, Stag's Leap Wine Cellars.

MAIN TOWNS Napa, St Helena, Calistoga.

AIRPORT San Francisco.

DAYS One to four.

BEST TIME TO GO

September to June.

SUMMARY Carneros – Yountville – Oakville – Rutherford – St Helena – Calistoga – Napa.

SOURCES OF INFORMATION

• *Napa Valley Vintners Association*
PO Box 141, St Helena,
CA 94574, USA.
Tel: +91 (707) 968-4201,
Fax: +91 (707) 963-3488.
Web: www.Napavintners.com

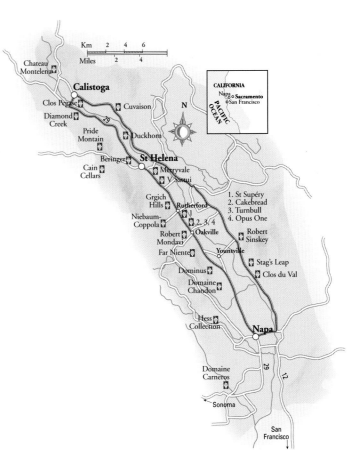

SONOMA

STEPHEN BROOK

In the 1960s it would have been difficult to predict that Sonoma County would become one of the most prestigious wine regions of California, with the ability to produce world-class wines from cabernet sauvignon, chardonnay and zinfandel grapes. Yet Sonoma has had a long history of wine production. A Hungarian, Agoston Haraszthy, planted vineyards at the Buena Vista estate in 1857, and in 1875 the county was producing 40 percent of all Californian wine, far outstripping neighboring Napa Valley in terms of production.

Napa was developed mostly by German immigrants such as Beringer, Schram and Krug. In contrast, Sonoma was colonized viticulturally by Italians, and many of their descendants are still there, as the names testify: Seghesio, Foppiano, Pedroncelli, and many more. But it was also a region where polyculture flourished, and well into the 1960s grape-farming families grew walnut trees, almonds, and pears. There were a few large old vineyards, such as Monte Rosso, but for the most part vineyards were small and family-owned.

The Napa renaissance began in the 1960s; Sonoma lagged behind, but has just about caught up. If Napa's strength is its relative homogeneity, Sonoma's is its diversity. Sonoma is much larger than Napa, its subregions more scattered, its vineyards more varied. That has made it harder for Sonoma to latch on to a clear identity for marketing purposes, as Napa has done successfully with cabernet. What's more, its proximity to San Francisco has meant that, more than Napa, it has succumbed to urban sprawl, as a drive up Highway 101 through Santa Rosa makes horribly clear. Many highly regarded vineyard sites of the 1970s are now shopping malls.

Although almost any grape variety will grow somewhere in Sonoma, certain regions are associated with specific varieties. Geyserville is famous for zinfandel, and Russian River Valley

LEFT Chateau St Jean, at the foot of Sugarloaf Ridge, is one of the largest wineries in Sonoma. Although the estate has 80 acres (32 hectares) of vineyards, additional grapes are bought in from other parts of the county.

produces some of California's finest pinot noir, while cabernet and merlot perform particularly well in Alexander Valley. So as you traverse the county you will be exposed to all kinds of varieties and styles. The Italian influence is strong and there are a number of wineries specializing in Italian varieties.

There are a large number of appellations in Sonoma and many of them overlap. It's useful to remember that a wine labelled Sonoma County is probably a blend from various parts of the county, whereas any other Sonoma appellation will have a more closely defined subregional origin.

Touring Sonoma is relaxing, although wineries close to San Francisco, in Carneros and the town of Sonoma itself, can get very crowded at weekends. In general, though, the atmosphere is more laid-back, and the wines slightly less expensive than in Napa.

Most visitors approach Sonoma from San Francisco, arriving via Highway 121, which crosses the cool Carneros region. One of the first wineries you come to, Viansa, produces Italian-style wines and foods – very welcome to wine lovers who are tired of the ubiquitous cabernet and chardonnay and would rather taste an arneis or barbera. A short distance up the road from Viansa, Cline specializes in Rhône varieties; their Ancient Vines bottlings are terrific. There are also excellent sparkling wines at Gloria Ferrer nearby.

Soon you will approach the charming little town of Sonoma. There are some good restored inns and bed and breakfast places here, making it an excellent base for visiting the southern part of the county. On the outskirts are some worthwhile wineries: Buena Vista is one of the oldest, but there are more exciting wines at Ravenswood, where the motto is 'No More Wimpy Wines.'

From the town, Route 12 leads through the Sonoma Valley towards Santa Rosa, a versatile growing region. Some wineries, such as Landmark, specialize in chardonnay, while

others, such as St Francis, have a fine range of merlot and cabernet sauvignon. One of the top wineries, Arrowood, has a good tasting room and well-trained staff. Other wineries to visit are Kunde, Kenwood and Château St Jean, which is best known for its lush chardonnays but also produces delicious reds.

Northwest of Santa Rosa is the Russian River Valley, which is prized for its pinot noir and chardonnay. Some of the small wineries here have won such a high reputation and sell out of their wines so fast that they no longer receive visitors. Among those that still maintain tasting rooms are Davis Bynum,

Rochioli, and DeLoach. The western part of Russian River is called Green Valley, and it is notoriously cool. Wineries here include Iron Horse, which makes delicious sparkling wines. If you keep heading west you will reach the Pacific Ocean, where vineyards planted high on the ridges overlooking the shore are generating a lot of excitement, especially for

Burgundian varieties. But unfortunately they are hard to find and not open to visitors.

Highway 101 heading north from Santa Rosa leads to Healdsburg, another excellent place to stay and to eat. Further north you come to Dry Creek Valley. This is zinfandel country, although other varieties flourish here too. Zinfandel is the only variety

Although Château Souverain in Geyserville, Alexander Valley, has been acquired by Australia's Mildara Blass group, it continues to produce a range of sensibly priced varietal wines.

indigenous to California and delivers rich spicy reds with supple tannins, port-style wines and a sweet pink abomination called white zinfandel or 'blush.' Some of the zinfandel vineyards are a hundred years old and give wines of amazing concentration of flavor. There are plenty of wineries here, and they all make pretty good wines. It's hard to go wrong at Seghesio, Pezzi King, Rafanelli, Quivira, and newcomer Yoakim Bridge.

At Preston there is a wide range of beautifully made and sensibly priced wines. Beyond Preston is one of Sonoma's showcase estates, Ferrari-Carano, where the wines are excellent and the gardens beautiful.

From here, continue on Highway 101 to Geyserville and Alexander Valley, one of the hottest regions in Sonoma. This is strictly red wine territory, although the large wineries buy in white grapes from other regions. Most of the wineries are close to the highway and geared for visitors, including Geyser Peak, Châteaux Souverain, and Simi.

Now, instead of returning south down Highway 101, head east to Highway 128, which connects Geyserville and Calistoga, taking you through Alexander Valley and then through Knights Valley, where there are quite a few vineyards but no wineries open to the public. This will take you to Calistoga and thus to Napa Valley; if you wish to avoid this, take 101 south from Geyserville towards San Francisco.

Most Sonoma wineries are in rural settings, making it an attractive option to picnic or just buy a bottle of wine and enjoy the view. If you need a break from wine tasting, it's not that far to the Pacific shore, where there are a number of resorts.

The Farmers' Market in Healdsburg is an outlet for the area's many vegetable and fruit growers, and local produce abounds in the restaurants, some of which are quite small, so booking is advisable, especially in summer. A few wineries, such as Topolos and Chateau Souverain, have their own restaurants, but the wine list can be limited. Try Bistro Ralph or the tiny Ravenous in Healdsburg, Café Lolo in Santa Rosa, and the rustic Willow Wood Café in Grafton. Often the only way to obtain sought-after Sonoma wines, such as a Kistler Chardonnay or a Rochioli Pinot Noir, is to order them from a restaurant wine list.

Visit Sonoma at any time. In summer only the most popular tasting rooms are crowded, and the harvest is too protracted for it to interfere with winery hospitality.

SONOMA

MAIN GRAPES

White: Chardonnay, sauvignon blanc.
Red: Cabernet sauvignon, merlot, syrah (shiraz), pinot noir, zinfandel.

LEADING APPELLATIONS (AVAS)

Carneros, Sonoma Valley, Sonoma Mountain, Chalk Hill, Russian River Valley, Green Valley, Dry Creek Valley, Alexander Valley, Sonoma Coast, Northern Sonoma.

MAIN PRODUCERS

Arrowood, Chateau St Jean, Chateau Souverain, Cline, DeLoach, Ferrari-Carano, Kenwood, Kunde, Landmark, Preston, Ravenswood, Simi, Stonestreet.

MAIN TOWNS

Sonoma, Santa Rosa, Healdsburg.

AIRPORT

San Francisco.

DAYS

Three to five days.

BEST TIME TO GO

Anytime.

SUMMARY

Sonoma – Glen Ellen – Santa Rosa – Healdsburg – Geyserville.

SOURCES OF INFORMATION

• *Sonoma County Wineries Association*
5000 Roberts Lake Rd, Rohnert Park, CA 94928, USA.
Tel: +91 (707) 586-3795.
Email: Info@sonomawine.com
Web: www.Sonoma.com

• *Russian River Valley Winegrowers*
875 Fulton Rd, Santa Rosa, CA 95439, USA.
Tel: +91 (707) 546-3276
Fax: +91 (707) 546-3277.

LEFT These gnarled zinfandel vines at the Pagani Ranch in Kenwood are over 100 years old, and yield rich, concentrated fruit.

CENTER The Russian River, which flows through one of California's best regions for pinot noir, is a popular recreation area.

RIGHT The main square at Healdsburg is filled with inns, restaurants, and wine shops that attract a steady stream of visitors throughout the year.

WASHINGTON AND OREGON

HILARY HADLEY-WRIGHT

The scent of pine forests in the air, birds of prey circling against a piercing blue sky, thundering rivers – not necessarily what you'd expect in wine country. Nor do vineyards commonly compete with hazelnut groves, apple orchards or hop gardens. The states of the Pacific Northwest offer contrasts rarely found in Europe and a vibrant sense of an emerging identity. This is new wine country, one that has seen exponential growth in the last decade.

A tour through the wine-growing regions of Washington and Oregon revives a sense of the pioneer spirit that created the American West. Unlike crowded European appellations, there is plenty of land ripe for vineyard planting, and at prices that entice vintners looking for more affordable plots. The spirit of the pioneers persists in a rugged individualism among growers who not only relentlessly experiment to discover which varieties work best where, but also support and encourage each other in a way that is rare in more established wine regions. This warmth extends to wine lovers, too. These are nearly all first-generation wineries, and visitors receive a warm welcome, maybe even from the person whose name is on the wine label. Many winemakers are happy to share their passion and excitement with others, which makes touring here a particularly pleasant experience.

Surprisingly, both Washington and Oregon receive more sunshine than California, with Washington's daily dose averaging 17.4 hours of summer sun, although the temperatures drop significantly at night. The extra couple of hours of sun, and the contrast between the hot days and cool nights, gives the grapes the chance to ripen slowly and gently, which provides them with an ideal balance between sugar and acidity.

LEFT At Oregon's Archery Summit, closely planted vineyards and gentle cellar handling yield stylish pinot noir in the Burgundian tradition. The cool climate of the Pacific Northwest favors pinot noir and chardonnay.

Winters can be severe, however, as the tall wind machines towering over many vineyards attest. These machines were mostly installed after the dramatic freeze of 1996, when temperatures dropped below the minimum tolerated by vines, leading to huge crop losses. The wind machines get the air moving, forcing it to circulate and disperse rather than sinking in freezing pockets, bringing death to the vines below. Although some wineries are open all year, you'll need to be confident with driving in heavy snow before you tackle the daunting Snoqualmie Pass over the Cascade mountains in winter to visit the vineyards in eastern Washington.

Many wineries in both states operate two annual 'open house weekends,' at Memorial Day (last weekend in May) and Thanksgiving (third Thursday in November). These are a perfect time to tour, as the wineries are really geared up for visitors, offering barrel samples, new releases, older vintages, and maybe even a free barbecue. Visitors can learn a lot, and it's a two-way street – many wineries value the feedback and exchange of information from customers who have visited several wineries and trawled through a wider-than-usual sample of local wines.

The route described in this tour is shaped like a figure '7.' Starting in Seattle it runs southeast through Washington to the vineyards of Yakima Valley and Walla Walla, then crosses into Oregon (which shares the Walla Walla appellation) and heads west along the stunning Columbia Valley gorge to Portland. From Portland the route turns south through the Willamette Valley, where most of Oregon's vineyards lie, and on to Umpqua and Rogue Valley. For many, the best way to do this tour will be to fly in via Seattle and out via Portland. These are both convivial cities with a refreshing approach to urban living, including witty public art and free public transport in the downtown area.

Seattle claims fame for the coffee revival, and both cities have many coffee houses, as well as brewpubs and microbreweries which take advantage of locally grown hops.

A visit to Seattle begins in the Pike Place market, source of more picnic food than you could possibly eat. Free entertainment is provided by juggling fishmongers touting their wares (they will ship salmon or crab home to many destinations, too). Pioneer Square, Seattle's birthplace, lies just a short stroll away. Recovered from a chequered past, it now houses some of the city's finest art galleries, antique shops and restaurants.

One of the delights of Seattle is that more than 25 wineries lie within easy reach of the city. The ferry terminal near Pike Place market offers a service to Bainbridge Island, home of the Puget Sound appellation or AVA (American Viticultural Area). Bainbridge Winery lies close to the arrival terminal and offers a pretty garden to picnic in.

Washington's wine region expands almost daily. In 1989 there were just 60 wineries, yet the state now boasts over 170. Wineries are opening at the rate of one every four or five weeks, and acreage under vine has doubled every four years. The resulting wines are winning major prizes, as the overall quality level is pretty high – but, sometimes, so are the prices – both here and in Oregon. Discretion is advised when buying, but there are exciting bargains to be had.

The northeastern suburb of Woodinville contains several excellent wineries, including Facelli, Château Ste Michelle (which hosts a superb summer concert season), DeLille and Columbia. You won't find more than a few token vines here, however, because location is one of the big decisions Washington winemakers must make. Should they live near their vineyards, 150 miles (240km) away in eastern Washington, or around Seattle, where

their customers are? Luckily, wine lovers can have their cake and eat it; some wineries are in Puget, the rest out east, which means that one can explore many Washington wineries without leaving the Seattle area.

Allow three hours for the journey east across the Snoqualmie Pass, with its dramatic mountain scenery, to the vineyards of Yakima, the Tri-Cities (Richland, Pascoe and Kennewick), which bask in around 300 days of sunshine a year in contrast to Seattle's 50, and Walla Walla. A few minutes from the highway, wineries such as Hogue or Hedges offer a warm welcome and a selection of well-made, well-priced wines. Walla Walla, in particular, contains several top-class wineries, with restaurants to match.

From Walla Walla the route heads west into Oregon along the stunning Columbia River Gorge. The pleasure of following the course of this stately river is one of the highlights of the trip, and worth allowing extra time for. Stop at the Bonneville Dam to watch salmon climb the fish ladder as they make their extraordinary journey back upriver to spawn. Local wild salmon is very popular with chefs in the region, its firm texture and deep flavor light-years away from the flabby farmed version.

Portland repays close exploration. It has a thriving farmers' market on Saturdays, an abundance of museums and galleries, and great boutique shopping in the Pearl district. Mix your own pinot noir blend at the Urban

RIGHT Viewed from 82 miles (130km) away, the 14,411ft (4400m) snow-covered Mount Rainier looms over summer vineyards near Zillah in the Yakima Valley AVA, Washington.

OPPOSITE Stop for a picnic at WillaKenzie Estate in Yamhill, Oregon, and enjoy panoramic views across the winery and vineyards, and the fresh country air.

Wine Works, or lose yourself in Powell's, which claims to be the world's largest new-and-second-hand bookshop. To fine-tune all the senses, take a trip to the International Rose Test Garden in Washington Park, where over 500 new varieties of roses are tested before being released for public cultivation.

The Willamette Valley is only an hour's drive from Portland, which means that basing yourself in the city is an option for a weekend visit. For longer stays, check out the many small bed and breakfasts in the valley.

Because of the distances involved, there is no signposted wine route but, armed with a good road map and the Wine Board's free winery guide, it is easy to find your way around. Should the effort of tasting prove too great, the dramatic Pacific coastline lies no more than an hour's drive away.

Willamette's 100 wineries offer plenty of choice, from biodynamic pinot noir at Cooper Mountain to rich pinot gris at WillaKenzie in Yamhill, where you can enjoy the spectacular view from the picnic area.

Further south, the wineries in the Umpqua and Rogue Valleys are more widely spaced, but the relative scarcity of visitors means an extra warm welcome. See the unique trellising system at King Estate, and taste sinuous tempranillo at Abacela Winery.

Eugene, Oregon's charming second city, has a lively atmosphere and a remarkable collection of fine restaurants, making it well worth a detour. Situated at the end of Rogue River Valley is Ashland, where the world-famous Shakespeare festival has an even longer season than the wineries.

ABOVE LEFT At Argyle Winery's tasting room on the main street through Dundee, Yamhill County, Oregon, you can sample excellent sparkling wine.
LEFT Abacela's proprietor, Earl Jones, examines young syrah vines protected by grow tubes in the newly planted Cobblestone Hill vineyard, Roseburg.

WASHINGTON AND OREGON

LEFT At Urban Wine Works in Portland, customers can test their winemaking skills by blending their own personal pinot noir from a range of different vintage and vineyard samples.

OREGON

MAIN GRAPES
Red: Pinot noir, merlot, cabernet sauvignon.
White: Pinot gris, chardonnay, riesling.

LEADING APPELLATIONS (AVAS)
Walla Walla Valley, Columbia Valley, Willamette Valley, Umpqua, Rogue, Applegate Valley.

MAIN PRODUCERS
Abacela Winery, Archery Summit Winery, Argyle Winery, Cooper Mountain, Henry Estate, King Estate, WillaKenzie Estate, Willamette Valley Vineyards.

WASHINGTON

MAIN GRAPES
Red: Merlot, cabernet sauvignon, syrah, cabernet franc, sangiovese, lemberger (limberger).
White: Chardonnay, riesling, sauvignon blanc, semillon.

LEADING APPELLATIONS (AVAS)
Yakima Valley, Walla Walla Valley, Columbia Valley, Puget Sound, Red Mountain.

MAIN PRODUCERS
Bainbridge Winery, Canoe Ridge, Château Ste Michelle, Chinook, Columbia Crest, Columbia, DeLille, Facelli, Hedges, Hogue, L'Ecole No. 41.

MAIN TOWNS
Seattle, Tri-Cities (Richland, Pascoe, Kennewick), Walla Walla.

AIRPORTS
Seattle-Tacoma (Seatac), Walla Walla.

DAYS
Four.

BEST TIME TO GO
April to October.

SUMMARY
Seattle – Woodinville – Ellensburg – Yakima – Tri-Cities – Walla Walla.

SOURCES OF INFORMATION
• *Washington Wine Commission*
104 Pike Street # 313, Seattle, WA 98101, USA.
Tel: +91 (206) 667-9463.
Web: www.washingtonwine.org

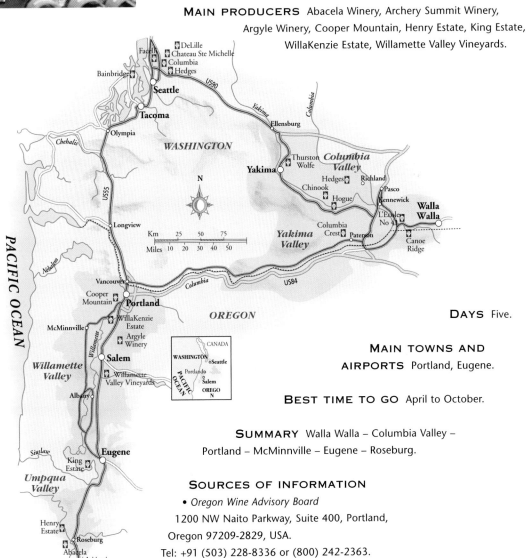

DAYS
Five.

MAIN TOWNS AND AIRPORTS
Portland, Eugene.

BEST TIME TO GO
April to October.

SUMMARY
Walla Walla – Columbia Valley – Portland – McMinnville – Eugene – Roseburg.

SOURCES OF INFORMATION
• *Oregon Wine Advisory Board*
1200 NW Naito Parkway, Suite 400, Portland, Oregon 97209-2829, USA.
Tel: +91 (503) 228-8336 or (800) 242-2363.
Web: www.oregonwine.org

SOUTH AUSTRALIA
McLAREN VALE

PETER FORRESTAL

For wine lovers, Adelaide is a great destination. Not only is it the capital of South Australia – the wine state, with 45 percent of the country's total wine production – but the city environs boast some of Australia's most alluring wine regions: Coonawarra, the Barossa Valley, the Clare Valley, Adelaide Hills, and the McLaren Vale. If you are in Adelaide with limited time on your hands, the dilemma is how to resolve the issue of which nearby wine region to visit: the deservedly popular, well-promoted and well-documented Barossa Valley; the picturesque Clare Valley with its increasingly respected riesling and shiraz; the emerging Adelaide Hills with its outstanding chardonnay, sauvignon blanc, and pinot noir; or the up-and-coming McLaren Vale, which is relatively unknown and under-promoted outside of the state.

The proximity of the McLaren Vale to Adelaide, which is less than an hour away, and the beaches along the Gulf of St Vincent, as well as its cozy, welcoming small wineries, or cellar doors, with their reliable wines and affordable prices, have made the McLaren Vale popular with locals who have long flocked to the region on weekends and during holiday periods.

Vines were planted in the McLaren Vale within a year of the establishment of the colony of South Australia in 1836 and, by 1880, the small number of vineyards in the area had developed a reasonable reputation in England for their deeply colored, full-bodied, alcoholic and tannic reds. The success of one local producer, Thomas Hardy, inspired significant expansion of the wine industry in the region between 1880 and 1910, and this period saw the foundation of several wineries which are familiar names today: Tatachilla, Amery, Piramimma, Wirra Wirra, and Mount Hurtle. During the first half of the 20th century, most wines from the area were sold

LEFT With a viticultural history that dates to 1864, family-owned Rosemount has vineyards in many areas, including this one in the McLaren Vale, where grapes for its renowned Balmoral Syrah are grown.

in bulk and bottled as multi-regional blends. This trend continues and many growers sell their grapes or bulk wine to producers outside the area. The local Winemakers Association has realized that this has hampered the growth of a regional identity, and they aim to have at least 80 percent of the area's wines branded as McLaren Vale by 2005.

Although these circumstances of history conspired to slow the growth of wine tourism in the region, things have been looking up in recent times. Most importantly, the ongoing rise of Australian shiraz over the past decade has placed the McLaren Vale firmly on the national and international stage. The robust, generously flavored shirazes that come from the region's warm climate have attracted consumers eager for good quality bargain reds, as well as wine lovers who are happy to pay high prices for top-class examples.

Large-scale investment in the McLaren Vale by some of Australia's major companies has resulted in some outstanding shirazes such as Rosemount's Balmoral, Brokenwood's Rayner Vineyard, and Tyrrell's Rufus Stone. BRL Hardy, which owns two of the region's oldest wineries, has evoked memories of the past with stunning reds under the Reynell and Tintara labels.

On a smaller scale, some revitalized local producers are sourcing fruit from very old vines and making some of the country's best shiraz, including Coriole Lloyd Reserve, d'Arenberg Dead Arm, Tatachilla Foundation, and Wirra Wirra RSW. Other producers, such as Noon, Clarendon Hills, Kay Brothers, and Fox Creek, are achieving cult status and steep prices for blockbuster shirazes that are well-oaked, deeply concentrated, high in alcohol and, sadly, in short supply.

While the search for a great shiraz might provide the impetus for visiting the McLaren Vale, wine lovers will find plenty more to delight them. Cabernet sauvignon, grenache, and grenache-shiraz blends tend to be big, rich, ripe, full-bodied, satisfying wines that are oaky and high in alcohol with generous flavors and velvety texture. The best whites come from the cooler parts of the region; chardonnay ranges from refined citrus to ripe, peachy characters, sauvignon blanc exhibits grassy, herbal, and tropical fruit flavors.

The changed status of the region's wines has affected the attitude of local vignerons towards tourism, but there is still diversity among the cellar doors (wineries open for visitors). Some are basic operations set up for the weekend trade from Adelaide, but an increasing number meet the expectations of national and international visitors.

OPPOSITE Undulating vineyards stretching to the the horizon are a feature of the McLaren Vale.

RIGHT Château Reynella, one of Australia's oldest wineries, was established in 1838 by John Reynell and remained in his family for over a century before it was acquired by the Hardy family in 1982. The old cellar (top), dug in 1845, is now covered with soil and turf. This building (below), dating from 1913, is now the headquarters of wine producer BRL Hardy.

The most significant development for wine tourism in the region was the opening, in 1997, of the McLaren Vale and Fleurieu Visitor Center, after local vignerons borrowed heavily to make a substantial contribution to its funding. In what must be a unique enterprise, they planted a 16 acre (6.5 hectare) vineyard in the surrounds of the Visitor Center; it now produces 4000 cases a year of Stump Hill Shiraz which is sold to raise funds. When the loan is paid off, the income from this wine will fund both the Center and the regional Winemakers Association. Ideally situated on the main road just before you reach the town of McLaren Vale, the Visitor Center provides general information about the region, takes accommodation bookings, and has a café, wine bar, and cellar door facilities offering tastings and sales for a number of the area's smaller wineries.

The McLaren Vale is easy to explore. It is divided by the Onkaparinga River and National Park. There are half a dozen wineries in the suburb of Reynella, including Geoff Merrill and Hardy's Château Reynella, one of South Australia's oldest and most historically important wineries. Most of the wineries are clustered around the town of McLaren Vale. To get there is a drive of less than an hour, mainly through suburban Adelaide along the Main South Road and the Victor Harbour Road. For a more circuitous, scenic route, you can drive via Blackwood, the Coromandel Valley, Clarendon and Kangarilla.

LEFT Situated in the main street of the township of McLaren Vale, these original cellars, completed in 1901, form part of the Tatachilla Winery operations.

Most of the 50-plus McLaren Vale wineries are small to medium-size operations and welcome visitors to their cellar doors. Apart from Coriole, no visit to the region is complete without calling at Chapel Hill, d'Arenberg, Edwards & Chaffey, Hardy's Tintara, Tatachilla, and Wirra Wirra. Other recommended wineries include Fox Creek, Geoff Merrill, Hardy's Reynella, Noon, Kay Brothers, and Woodstock.

It is possible to use Adelaide as a base for day trips to the McLaren Vale, but if you have two or three days, there are some terrific bed and breakasts in the region which will make your visit more relaxed and memorable. Start by calling at the Visitor Center to familiarize yourself with the area. The wineries are all within easy distance but it makes sense to plan a program around two groups: Chapel Hill, Edwards & Chaffey, Kay Brothers, and d'Arenberg; and Hardy's Tintara, Wirra Wirra, Tatachilla, and Fox Creek.

Combine your visits on one day with an energetic lunch at either Salopian Inn or d'Arry's Verandah. On the other day, spend a morning on or by the beach at Port Willunga or Aldinga; have lunch at the Star of Greece Café; check out Hamlet's Meat and Small Goods in High Street, Willunga; call in at Coriole; and finish in McLaren Vale with the McLaren Vale Olive Groves in Warner Road and Medlow Confectionery in Sand Road.

There's little that is glamorous about the region. But if you are in search of great shiraz, outstanding food, natural beauty and another aspect of the Australian experience, you'll find it all, and more, in the McLaren Vale.

Check the details of all of the above at the Visitor Center web site and don't be afraid to ask for help with your bookings.

Natural beauty takes on many forms in and around the McLaren Vale. At its western extremity lie broad, tranquil, sandy white beaches, tall stark cliffs and the natural coastal bushland of the Aldinga Scrub. Its boundaries are further defined by the windswept and hence ruggedly bare Sellicks Range which arc around and meet the dense bushland on the steep southern ranges of the Adelaide Hills. While the McLaren Flat has the lived-in feel of rural Australia, most of the Vale is gentle undulating country with a carefully wrought tapestry of vineyards, olive groves, stone fruit, almond and avocado orchards and natural bushland.

The McLaren Vale has a diversity of excellent, unpretentious places to eat. For many years, the Salopian Inn has been the quintessential Australian country restaurant, serving outstanding local produce, simply cooked. The Star of Greece Café has fabulous ocean views and serves the freshest seafood, skilfully prepared. d'Arry's Verandah is more formal, with a French influenced menu and sweeping views of the coastal plain – it's a place where you need to be prepared to linger. For coffee, a quick breakfast or light lunch, call at Market 190 on Main Street, McLaren Vale. Russell Jeavons' wood-fired pizza restaurant is only open on Friday nights and is always packed. Informality rules and the crowd (and Russell) dance into the night.

Coriole has long been one of the region's most innovative wineries and is worth a visit. As well as winemaking, it has been pressing top quality olive oil for years (three separate oils are now produced) and also makes some excellent vinegars. Recently they purchased Woodside, one of South Australia's best cheese companies. On Sunday afternoons, master baker John Downes produces sourdough loaves for an adoring public.

MAIN GRAPES

Red: Shiraz, cabernet sauvignon, grenache, merlot.
White: Chardonnay, sauvignon blanc, verdelho.

LEADING PRODUCERS

Chapel Hill, Clarendon Hills, Coriole, d'Arenberg, Geoff Merrill, Hardy's (Château Reynella, Tatachilla and Tintara), Noon, Kay Brothers, Wirra Wirra, Woodstock. (Some of the McLaren Vale's best shiraz is made by producers based elsewhere, notably Rosemount, Tyrrells and Brokenwood, who crush the grapes in the McLaren Vale and truck the must to the Hunter Valley.)

MAIN TOWNS   McLaren Vale, Adelaide.

NEAREST AIRPORT   Adelaide (about an hour's drive).

DAYS   Three.

BEST TIME TO GO   April to November.

SUMMARY   Carefully plan an itinerary or meander around the compact heart of the McLaren Vale for two to three days, seeking a balance between wine, food, and the natural beauty of the region.

SOURCES OF INFORMATION

• *McLaren Vale & Fleurieu Visitor Centre*
Main Road, McLaren Vale, South Australia 5171
Tel: +61 (8) 8223-9944.
Email: mclarenvale@visitorcentre.com.au
Web: www.visitorcentre.com.au

ABOVE LEFT Roman Bratasiuk's Clarendon Hills Winery at Blewitt Springs may be unprepossessing, but his wines have achieved cult status in the USA.

ABOVE RIGHT Chapel Hill's historic cellar door (wine tasting and sales center) was built in 1865 as the Christian Bible Church and parish school.

WESTERN AUSTRALIA
MARGARET RIVER

PETER FORRESTAL

The international reputation of Western Australian wines is a recent phenomenon, almost entirely a consequence of the quality of the chardonnays and cabernets coming from the Margaret River. Anyone visiting the west in search of its best wines will want to focus attention on its premium wine region, which is a most impressive destination for the wine tourist.

If you are looking for a comfortable, leisurely holiday in prime wine country, then you'll love spending a week in a world-class guesthouse, relaxing among the picturesque vineyards, beautifully situated cafés and the cellar doors (wineries open to visitors) of a thriving wine industry, or exploring the area's cottage industries, especially its art and craft galleries. The natural attractions are equally memorable: spectacular limestone caves, abundant bushland, tall forests, and magnificent surfing beaches. The lifestyle is quintessentially relaxed and easy-going, which should suggest the approach of the tourist wanting to get the most out of a visit.

The 167-mile (270-kilometer) drive south from Perth to Margaret River takes about three hours and is luxurious by local standards, with dual carriageway stretching for all but about 25 miles (40 kilometers) of the journey. The scenery on the way is unprepossessing: flat, low-lying coastal scrub relieved only by an occasional glimpse of water. Roads within the Margaret River region tend to be narrow and contain many bends or blind corners. Therefore caution needs to be exercised when driving. It is a solid one-hour drive from one extremity to the other and even visitors who are familiar with the area are invariably surprised by how widespread it is. There's a simple rule: any car journey takes longer than you expect. The alternative to driving is to take a one-hour charter flight from Perth to Margaret River.

LEFT The widely spaced vineyard rows at Cullen Wines in Wilyabrup overlook (from left) stone cottages which house the cellar door and a restaurant, the winery building, and the barrel store.

ABOVE LEFT Flutes Restaurant, overlooking the dam at Brookland Valley, is a tranquil lunch spot.

ABOVE RIGHT At Vasse Felix, the restaurant, tasting and sales are all housed in this cool subterranean room.

OPPOSITE Distant horizons, wide blue skies and sculptural gum trees are an integral part of the landscape of Western Australia; Cullen Wines, Wilyabrup.

Looking at the region today, it's hard to believe that in the 1960s Margaret River was a small, quiet rural community with a main street and a few basic stores. The local economy depended mainly on the dairy industry although there was also some beef cattle and potato farming and forestry. More than anything though, it is the grape which has changed the face of Margaret River in less than 30 years, and in the process built a reputation for the area as one of Australia's best wine regions and an internationally significant tourist destination.

Although responsible for not much more than one percent of the country's wine, the Margaret River produces a large percentage of Australia's premium wines – as much as 20 percent of the market that sells for US$12 or more a bottle. The cost of production is high, partly because yields throughout the region are low and partly because the vast majority of wineries are small, with a consequent impact on economies of scale.

The culture of the region was established by its earliest settlers who were inspired by a 1965 research report by Dr John Gladstone which suggested that the Margaret River had great viticultural potential. As a consequence, the first wave of pioneering winemakers, Tom Cullity (Vasse Felix 1967), Bill Pannell (Moss Wood 1969) and Kevin Cullen (Cullen 1971), planted in the Wilyabrup area; while David Hohnen (Cape Mentelle 1970) and Denis and Trisha Horgan (Leeuwin Estate 1974) chose to establish their vineyards closer to the town of Margaret River. All of these individuals were passionate about wine, regularly drank the benchmark wines of France, and were driven almost solely by a desire to produce great wine. Today, these wineries continue to set the standards and represent the pinnacle of winemaking achievement in the region.

The 1990s saw an exponential increase in wine quality, with chardonnays and cabernet sauvignons from Margaret River now regarded as among Australia's best examples of these varietals. The region's delicious fruity semillon-sauvignon blanc blends have also proved extremely popular on restaurant wine lists throughout Australia and overseas.

In the last decade, the landscape has been transformed by a dramatic increase in the number of vineyards planted, both by established wine companies and by growers. One unexpected side effect has been that the local kangaroo population has now reached plague proportions. Before their farms were replaced by vineyards, most farmers had culled kangaroos when their numbers rose beyond sustainable levels.

A recent move by companies such as Evans and Tate and Vasse Felix to establish vineyards in the flat, fertile, former potato-growing area of Jindong in the northeast of Margaret River has been criticized by some traditionalists who claim that the character of the wines from this part of the region will be radically different from those grown closer to the coast and further south.

The financial landscape is also changing in Margaret River. Devil's Lair is now owned by Southcorp, 50 percent of Brookland Valley by BRL Hardy, and Cape Mentelle by LVMH (Louis Vuitton-Moët Hennessy). Both Evans and Tate and Xanadu are publicly listed companies and are committed to rapid growth, while controversial newcomer Palandri has built up a large capital base from investors keen to take advantage of tax reduction. The economies of scale enjoyed by these larger companies has resulted in a greater range of entry level wines from them, but in some cases they have used grapes from outside the Margaret River to achieve this.

The sea is the greatest single geographical influence on the Margaret River wine region and the majority of its vineyards are within 3 miles (5 kilometers) of the Indian Ocean. The climate is the most maritime-influenced of any Australian wine region, with the lowest mean annual temperature around 46°F (8°C), and a long, dry period from October to April, during which only 8in (200mm) of rain may fall. Most of the prime viticultural land is on gently undulating slopes. The dominant soil type is gravelly or gritty sandy loam formed from granite and gneissic rock. As sloping sites tend to lose moisture quickly, many vignerons believe there is a need for irrigation to supplement water supplies.

The Roaring Forties are strong westerly winds that are responsible for the region's fabulous surf as well as one of its major viticultural problems: the fresh salty winds in spring which affect budburst and keep yields low (especially with chardonnay).

The beach culture of Dunsborough, Yallingup, Gracetown, and Margaret River has been long established and the annual influx of holidaymakers from Perth continues to give definition to the summer scene in the area. There are some 80 miles (130 kilometers) of rugged coastline stretching from Cape Naturaliste to Cape Leeuwin, featuring pristine sandy beaches, towering granite outcrops and battered limestone cliffs. Several sites provide consistent, spectacular, world-class surfing all year round, with Margaret River being the venue for the International Coca-Cola Masters in the fall. Many of the region's winemakers were first attracted to Margaret River by the lure of the surf and, at least in the early days, there were apocryphal stories of pickers disappearing when the surf was up.

As the word spread about the quality of Margaret River wines in the late 1970s and 1980s, Western Australians started to visit wineries on their trips south. The local vignerons saw this as a lucrative way to market their wines and many established cellar doors (tasting and sales facilities) to meet demand. With the rise in visitor numbers in the 1990s, winery restaurants and more classy, stylish cellar doors became an increasingly important means of attracting larger numbers of tourists. Most impressive of the cellar doors are Brookland Valley, Cape Mentelle, Cullen, Howard Park, Leeuwin, Vasse Felix, and Voyager.

There are outstanding, newly renovated restaurants and stable kitchen brigades (delicatessen counters) at Vasse Felix, Leeuwin and Cullen. Here the food tends to follow the modern Australian brasserie style of fresh, light and simple dishes using quality ingredients, often with an emphasis on local produce. There are also good to very good cafes at Brookland Valley, Amberley, Voyager, Clairault, and Wise Winery.

In planning a tour of the region, you should consider spending two or three days in the locality of Wilyabrup, a day around Margaret River (sometimes called the Wallcliffe subregion), and a day near Yallingup. The greatest concentration of excellent wineries is in the Wilyabrup Valley, where Cullen, Pierro, Vasse Felix, and Howard Park should not be missed. Lenton Brae, Brookland Valley, Evans and Tate, Hay Shed, Hill and four revitalized properties – Ribbon Vale, Gralyn, Juniper, and Arlewood – are also worthy of serious consideration.

In the Wallcliffe locale, Cape Mentelle is the most quintessentially 'Margaret River' of the wineries; Voyager is grand, and Leeuwin provides a classy echo of the Napa. While the experience of visiting each is dramatically different, all three make outstanding wines. Consider, too, calling in at the dynamic, expansionist Xanadu, and the unsung, quiet achiever Redgate.

Find time to drive south on Caves Road to experience the almost mystical Boranup Forest. While in Margaret River, stop at the Urban Bean in the main street for a coffee or a light lunch, or at the Margaret River Pottery and Art Galleries to satisfy your artistic urges.

Amberley is the best wine producer near Yallingup. With its carefully manicured lawns and meticulously maintained vineyard set against a backdrop of natural bushland, it makes for a tranquil, relaxing visit. Three other cellar doors in the area add value in quite different ways. Wise offers spectacular views of the sea at Geographe Bay, Happs an adjacent pottery studio, and Clairault a stylish café. Use this day to check out the local beaches, call on two of the region's best art galleries (Gunyulgup and Yallingup) and stop for an ice cream at Simmo's.

Among the reasons for the popularity of Margaret River is that it offers so much in addition to wine tourism. Some of the most spectactular local sights are the limestone caves, Jewel, Lake, Moondyne, Mammoth, and Ngilgi, which were formed more than two millon years ago. Moondyne is an adventure cave but all the others have safely railed steps and paths. Jewel is the most stunning, with the world's longest straw stalactite, a Tasmanian tiger fossil and impressive formations highlighted by cleverly placed lighting. Strongly recommended for the adventurous is the four-hour Cave and Canoe Bushtucker tour, while the faint of heart would probably prefer the more luxurious option of being chauffeured around the region by Nola Gaebler in a restored Bentley. For more information and bookings contact the Augusta Margaret River Tourist Bureau.

LEFT Damage is substantially reduced at harvest when the marris (red gum trees) blossom, as birds prefer them to the grapes.

MARGARET RIVER

ABOVE Prevelly Beach, at the mouth of the Margaret River, is safe, but some local beaches can be dangerous. Many of the region's winemakers are avid surfers who revel in the world-class waves.
CENTER Kangaroos are not loved by grape farmers, as young vine shoots are a favorite snack. Culling, once permitted, is now prohibited, and the kangaroo population is rising.
RIGHT Harvesting zinfandel grapes at Cape Mentelle, a property in the Louis Vuitton-Moët Hennessy (LVMH) group. Hand-picking ensures that only ripe bunches are taken.

MAIN GRAPES
White: Chardonnay, semillon, sauvignon blanc, verdelho.
Red: Cabernet sauvignon, merlot, shiraz.

LEADING PRODUCERS
Cape Mentelle, Clairault, Cullen, Devil's Lair, Evans and Tate, Howard Park, Leeuwin Estate, Lenton Brae, Moss Wood, Pierro, Vasse Felix, Voyager Estate, Xanadu, Amberley, Brookland Valley, Palandri, Sandalford.

MAIN TOWNS
Margaret River, Dunsborough, Yallingup, Cowaramup.

AIRPORT
Perth. (There is no regular service to Margaret River, although charter flights are available from Perth.)

DAYS
Five.

BEST TIME TO GO
April to November.

SUMMARY
Use Margaret River or Wilyabrup as a base. It's a solid one-hour drive from one extremity of the region to the other. Spend two to three days in Wilyabrup and a day each in the Yallingup and Wallcliffe areas.

SOURCES OF INFORMATION
• *Augusta Margaret River Tourism Association*
Tel: + 61 (8) 9757-2911.
Email: amrta@netserv.net.au
Web: www.margaretriverwa.com

1. Wise
2. Happs
3. Amberley Estate
4. Clairault
5. Moss Wood
6. Lenton Brae
7. Evans & Tate
8. Sandalford
9. Brookland Valley
10. Pierro
11. Hay Shed Hill
12. Cullen
13. Arlewood
14. Howard Park
15. Vasse Felix
16. Juniper Estate
17. Palandri
18. Cape Mentelle
19. Xanadu
20. Voyager Estate
21. Leeuwin Estate
22. Devil's Liar

MARLBOROUGH

AND THE SOUTH ISLAND

ROSEMARY GEORGE MW

Although the oldest existing winery in New Zealand dates from 1851, the modern era really began in 1973, in Marlborough, when Frank and Mate Yukich, the then owners of Montana, planted the first sauvignon blanc vines in the South Island. Some wine had been made previously in the region, but certainly nothing of note. 1980 saw the first commercial vintage of Marlborough sauvignon blanc and it simply took off, capturing the imagination and tastebuds of wine drinkers, not just in New Zealand, but all over the world. We were given a brand-new flavor, quite unlike any sauvignons from anywhere else, and we were captivated.

This makes Marlborough as good a place as any to start a tour of the South Island. Small Metroliner aircraft, too low to stand up in, fly across the Cook Strait from Wellington into Blenheim airport. The view of the Kaikoura Range when you land is the same one that inspired the evocative label of Cloudy Bay, one of the region's best-known wines. On a clear day, the views over the Marlborough Sounds are fabulous, but on a windy day the short hop becomes a battle of nerves and stomach. An alternative is the slower, but not necessarily smoother, ferry from Wellington, for the Cook Strait is not known for its calm waters. Again the views as you come down the Marlborough Sounds into the harbor at Picton make a wonderful introduction to the South Island. Base yourself in Blenheim, the center of the wine region and a cheerful, bustling town with large signs on the outskirts proudly boasting New Zealand's sunniest city. There is a choice of hotels, of which Hotel D'Urville is the smartest. Outside the town, bed and breakfasts, what New Zealanders call a 'home stay', offer a friendly alternative.

LEFT Rippon Vineyards on the shore of Lake Wanaka in Central Otago has one of the most spectacular vineyard views in the world. Rolfe Mills, a wine pioneer of the region, first planted vines here in 1976.

Distances between wineries are small, with the Wairau Valley now densely planted with vines. After Montana, Te Whare Ra, Hunter's and Cloudy Bay were the next wineries to explore the potential of Marlborough. Since then new wineries and labels have followed at such a breathtaking rate that Marlborough is now the largest wine-producing region in the country, and land that was once sheep grazing pasture has been transformed into vast tracts of vineyards.

Most New Zealand wineries welcome visitors, often much more so than in many parts of the Old World. They are well-signposted and easy to find. Throughout the summer, most wineries are open on a daily basis, usually from Labor Day (late October) to the Easter weekend, and will provide a tasting, for which you may have to pay. For cellar tours, though, you may need to phone ahead for an appointment. Some of the larger wineries also have restaurants, often offering stylish cuisine and the opportunity to dine with a view of the vines and the surrounding hills. Winery restaurants include Allan Scott, Montana, Hunter's, Wairau River, and Domaine Georges Michel, where you can drink Beaujolais as well as sauvignon blanc. There may even be an art exhibition or concert to tempt the visitor.

It is the Wairau River that accounts for the terroir (total natural environment) of the area. The vineyards are planted on stony free-draining soils of the valley floor, with the stones reflecting the sunshine during the day and retaining warmth during the night. As there is little soil to retain water, irrigation is often necessary. Running parallel to the broad Wairau Valley is the narrower Awatere Valley. Vavasour, the first winery here, was planted in 1986, and since then others have followed. The drive through the Wither hills over the Dashwood Pass offers some fine views and, maybe, even a glimpse of a hawk.

Sauvignon blanc may be synonymous with Marlborough, but the region offers much else besides. Other aromatic grape varieties, such as riesling and gewürz-traminer, perform well here and there is an increasing interest in pinot gris.

Chardonnay is almost invariably fermented and aged in wood, producing ripe buttery flavors with a fresh acidity. It is also invaluable for the growing sparkling wine industry, which has benefited from overseas expertise and investment. Deutz Champagne created Cuvée Deutz in conjunction with Montana; Veuve Clicquot's involvement in Cloudy Bay has helped perfect Pelorus; while

LEFT Scott Henry trellising, with its divided canopy, helps control vigor, a perennial problem for New Zealand viticulture; Dog Point Vineyard, Cloudy Bay.
OPPOSITE What better way to enjoy the scenery of the Wairau Valley than a balloon trip over Brancott, Montana's flagship vineyard?

Hunter's Mirumiru, meaning 'bubbles' in Maori, is advised by Domaine Chandon in Australia. It was a *champenois*, Daniel le Brun, who started the first winery in New Zealand dedicated to sparkling wine alone.

Blenheim enjoys long sunshine hours, but it is not always warm enough to ripen cabernet sauvignon and merlot. There is no doubt that in the South Island, pinot noir is more successful than the Bordeaux varieties. Pinot noir tends to be a temperamental grape that is extremely demanding in its growing conditions and vinification methods, but over the last decade, winemakers from Martinborough (the southernmost vineyard area of the North Island) southwards, have been succeeding in their challenge to make pinot noir with convincing varietal flavors.

The best New Zealand pinot noirs now rival the finest from California or Oregon and often taste better than an average village Burgundy. Some of the earlier plantings were of less satisfactory clones but now the choice is greater. Of course, like chardonnay, it is a vital component of sparkling wine.

Nelson is separated from Marlborough by hills. There is a winding road from Blenheim, with stunning scenery and little traffic, or you can fly to Nelson from Wellington. Nelson was named after the admiral as a twin to Wellington, across the Cook Strait. Today it is known for its arts and crafts, with potters attracted by the local clays. Leave the town behind you and drive west into the gentle rolling countryside of the Waimea Plains.

For several years, Nelson was dominated by just two wineries, Seifried Estate and Neudorf, but recently wine production here has gathered momentum. Nelson will never attain the scale of Marlborough, and it retains a delightful off-the-beaten-track backwater feel about it, but nonetheless there is much to engage the tourist, including one of the country's best winemakers. Tim Finn at Neudorf has a way with chardonnay, and his

LEFT Gibbston Valley's vineyard on the outskirts of Queenstown, Central Otago, was planted in 1981. The climate here is similar to Burgundy's Côte d'Or.

hills to the snow-capped Southern Alps, with new plantings of vines lining the flat valley floor. Fine riesling was first planted here by the Giesen brothers who hail from Germany, and others have followed their example. Pinot noir is also establishing a reputation here. Enjoy it overlooking the delightful Pegasus Bay, or at the winery restaurant at Waipara Springs, where you can enjoy home-grown fresh asparagus in season.

If time permits, you can drive on further to the world's most southerly vineyards, on the 45th parallel in Central Otago. It takes five hours to drive to Wanaka, but on a clear day you will be rewarded with breathtaking views of New Zealand's highest mountain, Aoraki/Mt Cook. Alternatively, if time is short, fly from Christchurch to Queenstown.

The early pioneers of viticulture in Central Otago were considered quite mad, but, contrary to all expectations, it is now the fastest-growing wine region in New Zealand. There are vineyards in the Gibbston Valley outside Queenstown, around the old gold-mining towns of Cromwell and Alexandra, and the solitary Rippon Vineyards on Lake Wanaka, with its wonderful views of the lake and the dramatic skyline of the Buchanan mountains. Pinot noir flourishes in Central Otago where the numerous wineries which have established a reputation for this variety include Gibbston Valley Wines, Chard Farm, Felton Road, Mount Edward, Quartz Reef, and Rippon Vineyards.

Here, as elsewhere in the South Island, the long hours of summer daylight seem to enhance the fruit flavors of not just pinot noir, but of other varieties too, showing just how much New Zealand deserves its reputation as a fine wine producer.

riesling and pinot noir have much to recommend them too. The winery restaurant is open during January and there is also picnic space available next to the lovely weatherboard buildings. Ruby Bay, with views over the eponymous bay, is the most picturesque winery of the region.

From Blenheim, drive south down the coast road, looking over the Pacific Ocean, and maybe stopping for fresh lobster in Kaikoura if the season is right, and you will come to the very English city of Christ-church. The river Avon, lined with willow trees, meanders through the city center. The first British settlers arrived here in 1850, but the region's first vines were already there, brought by the French when they landed at Akaroa, on Banks Peninsula, in 1840.

Today there are just a few wineries on the Canterbury Plains outside Christchurch and a couple more on Banks Peninsula. However, Waipara, a river valley surrounded by hills, some 40 minutes' drive north of the city, is really the place to visit. Although cool, the climate in Waipara is distinctly warmer than on the Canterbury Plains and, unusually for New Zealand, limestone forms the basis of the soil, with layers of silt loam.

The view from the summit of Mount Cass provides a magnificent panorama over the

ABOVE LEFT Visitors to Gibbston Valley Wines can take a tour through the 250ft (76-meter-long) underground cave that is lined with barrels of maturing chardonnay and pinot noir.

ABOVE RIGHT Neudorf Vineyards in Upper Moutere, Nelson. The village's many oak trees are thought to have been planted by German settlers in the early 1840s.

MAIN GRAPES

Red: Pinot noir, cabernet sauvignon, merlot.
White: Sauvignon blanc, chardonnay, riesling, pinot gris, gewürztraminer.

LEADING AREAS AND PRODUCERS

Nelson: Greenhough Vineyard, Neudorf Vineyard, Ruby Bay Winery, Seifried Estate.
Marlborough: Allan Scott Wines, Cloudy Bay, Fromm Winery, Grove Mill, Huia Vineyards, Hunter's Wines, Isabel Estate, Jackson Estate, Montana, Seresin, Villa Maria Estate, Vavasour Wines, Wairau River.
Canterbury: Giesen Wine Estate.
Waipara: Canterbury House, Daniel Schuster Wines, Pegasus Bay, Waipara Springs, Waipara West.
Central Otago: Chard Farm, Felton Road, Gibbston Valley Wines, Mount Edward, Quartz Reef, Rippon Vineyard.

MAIN TOWNS AND AIRPORTS

Marlborough: Nelson, Blenheim.
Waipara: Christchurch.
Central Otago: Queenstown.

DAYS Seven, excluding Central Otago.

BEST TIME TO GO October to March.

SUMMARY Marlborough – Nelson – Waipara – Central Otago.

SOURCES OF INFORMATION

• *Marlborough Tourist Office*
PO Box 29, Blenheim, Marlborough, New Zealand.
Tel: +64 (3) 577-5520, Fax: +64 (3) 577-5530.
Email: Dest.Marlborough@xtra.co.nz
Web: www.destination.marlborough.com

Due to the large area covered by this tour, only Marlborough is shown in detail.

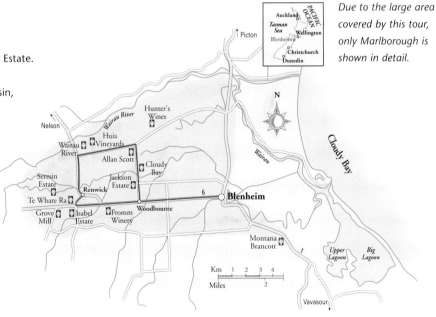

STELLENBOSCH

AND FRANSCHHOEK

WENDY TOERIEN

The heart of the Cape winelands lies about 30 miles (50 kilometers) east of Cape Town, in Stellenbosch, Paarl, Somerset West, and the Franschhoek valley. These are among the most beautiful of the world's wine-producing regions, where craggy mountain peaks overlook vine-covered slopes, and undulating hills roll down towards False Bay. Against the myriad greens of forested kloofs and intensively cultivated land lies the contrast of white buildings, from grandly gabled Cape Dutch homesteads to humble, whitewashed workers' cottages.

The region's viticultural history dates from the late 17th century, when the governors of the fledgling Cape Colony, founded in 1652, dispatched Dutch and French settlers, many of them grape growers, inland to extend the colony's boundaries. Today's wine makers still have strong ties to their viticultural heritage, but the traditional emphasis on classic varieties and minimal cellar manipulation is being balanced by modern vineyard practices and vinification techniques.

The Cape's Mediterranean climate, with mild, rainy winters and long, warm dry summers, is ideal for growing grapes. The south and southeast-facing mountain slopes, which catch cooling breezes from the Atlantic Ocean 15 to 9 to 12 miles (20 kilometers) away, are ideal for sauvignon blanc and pinot noir, while cabernets sauvignon and franc, merlot, and pinotage are grown on the lower, warmer, north-northeast-facing slopes. Other varieties grown in the Cape include shiraz, chardonnay, and chenin blanc, South Africa's most widely planted grape.

Most wineries are open for tasting and sales Monday to Friday and Saturday mornings, with a few open on Saturday afternoons and Sundays. Cellar tours are usually by appointment only.

LEFT Boschendal, at the entrance to the Franschhoek valley, is popular with visitors, who come for the 17th-century traditional Cape architecture, fine local cuisine and a classic range of red, white, and sparkling wines.

Leaving Cape Town behind you, take the N1 towards Paarl, turning onto the R44 in the direction of Franschhoek. Make your first stop at Glen Carlou, a joint venture between Walter Finlayson and Californian Donald Hess of the Hess Collection in the Napa Valley. Nowadays, Walter concentrates on farm cheesemaking, leaving winemaker son David to turn out the gorgeous chardonnays which are so much in demand in the USA, a Bordeaux-style 'classic claret,' pinot noir and merlot as well as Cape Vintage, a traditional Portuguese-style port.

Continue on to Franschhoek, a picture-perfect valley of vines and fruit orchards nestled in the wrap-around Klein Drakenstein mountains. Capitalizing on its heritage (the name means 'French corner'), this colorful little village has a deserved reputation as the Cape's culinary center, where French and Mediterranean influences combine with Malay spices and traditional farm fare. Seek out local specialties such as succulent Karoo lamb, tender ostrich, freshly caught rainbow trout and farm cheeses. Combine stylish accommodation with fine food at Le Quartier Français, La Couronne, La Petite Ferme or Monneaux Franschhoek Country House. In July, the town celebrates Bastille Day with food, festivities and, of course, wine.

At Cabrière Estate the owner, exuberant Prussian baron Achim von Arnim, regales visitors with the magic of traditional *méthode champenoise* production. His Pierre Jourdan range of Cap Classiques (the local term for bottle fermented bubblies) and a fruity, truffle-like pinot noir are matched with specific dishes at Haute Cabrière, a hillside restaurant up the Franschhoek Pass.

For rich reds, visit opulent La Motte where a Huguenot heritage (it dates from the 1700s) and commitment to classic viticulture are evident in the flagship Bordeaux-blend, Millennium (named well before the much-hyped event!), a benchmark shiraz and an elegant chardonnay.

On the other side of the town, secluded Boekenhoutskloof, a mere decade old, leans firmly toward the Côte Rôtie with its densely fruited shiraz (labeled Syrah here). A claret-like cabernet sauvignon and a smoothly oaked semillon (a variety synonymous with Franschhoek) also feature. A second label, Porcupine Ridge, made for easier drinking, has proved popular in London restaurants.

With more than 20 wineries, almost all of which offer tastings and cellar tours, allow at least two days to fully explore Franschhoek.

For lovers of Cape wine, however, it is Stellenbosch that demands one's attention. Leaving Franschhoek behind, take the R310, the intriguingly named Helshoogte Pass (hell's heights), over the Simonsberg range.

ABOVE New vineyards take shape on the foothills of Franschhoek's Drakenstein Mountains as the valley's wine-growing status soars.

OPPOSITE LEFT At Cabrière, pinot noir and an aperitif wine, Petit Pierre Ratafia, are matured in the vaulted barrel cellar overlooked by the restaurant.

OPPOSITE RIGHT Stellenbosch's Kanonkop is aptly signposted by an old cannon (*kanon*), which used to alert the fledgling colony's farmers to the arrival of provision-bearing ships in distant Table Bay.

At the turn-off is Boschendal, a visitors' favorite with its Cape Dutch manor house museum, restaurants and glamorous new winery offering tastings and cellar tours. Stop here for lunch, but book in advance for the popular Cape buffet, held in the original cellar, or Le Pique-Nique (prepacked hampers to enjoy in the gardens in summer).

After ascending the winding pass, turn in at Thelema Mountain Vineyards for a taste of the multi award-winning, fruit-rich cabernet sauvignon, merlot, sauvignon blanc, and chardonnay produced by the laid-back, irrepressible yet dedicated Gyles Webb. Local and international demand keeps these wines in short supply, even more so after the loss of some vines to raging mountain fires in 2000.

Drive through the tranquil suburbs of Stellenbosch to the Jonkershoek Valley, home to Neil Ellis, a négociant vintner dedicated to top quality winemaking. Grapes sourced from growers in different areas are used for the Stellenbosch, Groenekloof, and Elgin ranges, and single-vineyard wines are bottled under a Reserve Vineyard Selection label.

Across town, in Ida's Valley, the historic Rustenberg Estate (est. 1683), nestles among oak trees beneath the majestic Simonsberg. The gracious Cape Dutch homestead is juxtaposed with a hi-tech cellar and tasting room, the result of a multimillion-rand makeover in the 1990s. Seek out the highly rated Peter Barlow or standard Rustenberg, the first a 100 percent cabernet sauvignon and the second a classic Bordeaux blend.

There is a wide range of accommodation in and around Stellenbosch and many wine farms have upmarket guesthouses or bed and breakfasts. Make time to explore the historic town center on foot. Founded by Simon van der Stel in 1679, it is now the hub of the Cape winelands. A university town, it has narrow, oak-lined streets that bustle with students in term-time, which has generated a lively arty pavement café and pub society. Wander along Dorp Street, with its restored Cape Dutch and Victorian buildings, art galleries, antique shops, restaurants and coffee houses, calling at Oom Samie se Winkel, a reminder of the general-dealer stores of old.

Turning back to the winelands, take the R44 west of the town. Here, on the slopes of the Simonsberg, lies Kanonkop, with its burly, outspoken winemaker of 30 years, Beyers Truter, the champion of South Africa's indigenous red variety, pinotage, in all its intensely fruited, heavily wooded, tannic glory. This is old Cape winemaking – with a New World slant – at its best. A red blend under the Paul Sauer label and a cabernet sauvignon complete a trio of blockbusters that have earned him international awards.

On the same road are L'Avenir, where Francois Naudé produces bold ripe reds and mouthfilling chardonnay and chenin blanc; and Warwick, where Norma Ratcliffe proved that winemaking was not a job just for the boys. Her cabernet franc (one of the few local examples), flagship Bordeaux-blend Trilogy, and elegant chardonnay consistently win acclaim at home and abroad.

Return to Stellenbosch on the same road, stopping for lunch at gracious Morgenhof, with its unusual combination of restored Cape Dutch and classical French architecture, and a circular underground barrel-maturation cellar *à la* Château Lafite-Rothschild. Owner Anne Cointreau-Huchon (of the Cognac-based Cointreau family) and talented young wine maker Rianie Strydom form a dynamic duo, producing an extensive range that includes luscious merlots, fresh chardonnays, and an elegant Cap Classique bubbly.

The next day, head eastwards to the Helderberg, stopping at three small boutique wineries. At Waterford, a stylish stone cellar,

shiraz is the flagship, but the chardonnay, sauvignon blanc, and cabernet sauvignon also exhibit winemaker Kevin Arnold's trademark elegance. Grangehurst's Jeremy Walker makes intense pinotages, cabernets, and merlots in blended and single-varietal versions. High on the slopes at Cordoba, Chris Keet makes his acclaimed cabernet franc-based Crescendo.

Break for lunch at the succinctly named 96 Winery Road, where the wine list offers wines from Helderberg 'and the rest of the

world.' Restaurant owner Ken Forrester's own barrel-fermented chenin blanc makes an ideal match for the country cuisine on the menu.

Divide your final day between two of the Cape's finest wine properties. Both are steeped in history, but the first reflects the brave new world of modern Cape viticulture, while the second retains traditional elegance.

Vergelegen's hi-tech, octagonal, multi-level cellar sunk into a hill overlooking the town of Somerset West, is the domain of often controversial, but undeniably talented, winemaker André van Rensburg, whose objective is to make his wines among the best in the world. Vines were first planted here in 1700, but today's show-stopping wines come from vineyards planted since 1989. Lunch at the Lady Philips Restaurant or Rose Terrace, and stroll through Vergelegen's immaculately restored Cape Dutch buildings or the gardens with their centuries-old camphor trees.

Backtracking towards Cape Town, end your tour at Meerlust, a three-century-old Cape 'first growth' of enduring quality, where eighth-generation owner Hannes Myburgh and his winemaker of two decades, Italian-born Giorgio Dalla Cia, produce sought-after wines that are the very essence of elegance, including Rubicon, the estate's signature cabernet sauvignon-based blend, a pinot noir, chardonnay, and a merlot. Tasting is by appointment only and includes a cellar tour.

In Stellenbosch, stay at D'Ouwe Werf, a converted 19th-century inn in the heart of the town, the elegant Lanzerac Hotel, a Cape Dutch manor with its own winery, or the cozy Devon Valley Hotel; or choose from a variety of guesthouse or bed and breakfast options. Somerset West offers Willowbrook Lodge, a member of the Relais & Châteaux group.

BELOW Vergelegen's modern hilltop winery utilizes gravity flow and the latest in cellar technology to ensure minimum handling of the grapes.

MAIN GRAPES

Red: Cabernet sauvignon, merlot, cabernet franc, shiraz, pinotage, pinot noir.

White: Sauvignon blanc, chardonnay, chenin blanc, semillon.

LEADING AREAS AND PRODUCERS

(*This is just a small selection. A good guide book is essential.*)

Franschhoek: La Motte, Cabrière Estate, Boschendal, Boekenhoutskloof.

Stellenbosch: Thelema, Neil Ellis, Rustenberg, Kanonkop, Morgenhof, L'Avenir, Warwick.

Helderberg: Waterford, Grangehurst, Cordoba, Vergelegen, Meerlust.

MAIN TOWNS Cape Town, Franschhoek, Stellenbosch, Somerset West.

AIRPORT Cape Town.

DAYS Six.

BEST TIME TO GO October to April.

SUMMARY Franschhoek – Stellenbosch (Jonkershoek, Simonsberg) – Somerset West (Helderberg).

ABOVE LEFT At Thelema Mountain Vineyards, meticulous viticulture builds the base for sought-after, award-winning wines.

ABOVE RIGHT Rustenberg's elegant, gabled homestead reflects the estate's enduring status as one of the Cape's premier properties.

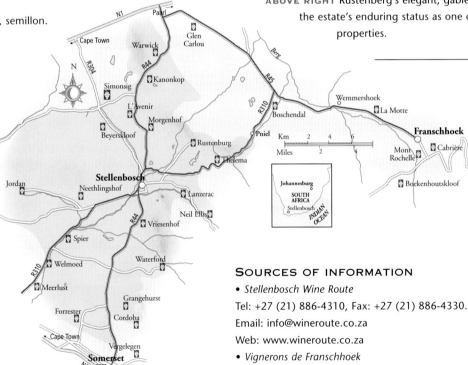

SOURCES OF INFORMATION

• *Stellenbosch Wine Route*
Tel: +27 (21) 886-4310, Fax: +27 (21) 886-4330.
Email: info@wineroute.co.za
Web: www.wineroute.co.za

• *Vignerons de Franschhoek*
Tel: +27 (21) 876-3062, Fax: +27 (21) 876-2974.
Email: franschhoek@wine.co.za
Web: www.franschhoekwines.co.za

CONSTANTIA,
ELGIN AND WALKER BAY

WENDY TOERIEN

From the verdant valley of Constantia, into the mountains of Elgin and across the patchwork landscape of the Overberg wheatfields to the maritime Walker Bay environs, this trip through some of South Africa's finest cool-climate and coastal vineyards moves from the historic core of the Cape's viticultural heritage to some pioneering, new-wave wineries.

Dutch colonial governor Simon van der Stel was granted Groot Constantia estate in 1685. Vines still flourish in the Constantia valley, just 20 minutes' drive from Cape Town, but the land has become sought-after real estate, and only a small 990 acre (400 hectare) pocket of vineyards survives amid suburban sprawl. Yet scenic sprawl it is, with treed gardens and verdant verges, horse paddocks and bridle paths, and views of the Atlantic Ocean from the south-facing Constantiaberg hills. Classic cool-climate sauvignon blanc, pinot noir, and weisser (Rhine) riesling come from the high-lying granite and sandstone slopes, while cabernet sauvignon, merlot, cabernet franc, shiraz, and pinotage emerge from sandier soils lower down. Historically, wine producers in South Africa catered for all tastes, making a wide range of wines rather than concentrating on just one or two varieties, but the new trend is for specialization.

Groot Constantia is the ideal first stop. The farm and its historic buildings are managed by a trust as a public venture and it's a popular tourist spot. The Cape Dutch manor house is a museum of fine colonial furniture and homeware, and the old wine cellar recalls winemaking days of yore. The massive modern winery produces some 45,000 cases annually, mostly from classic grape varieties. The cellar is open for conducted tours, including an audio-visual presentation, for which a fee is charged, and there's a popular tavern for lunch.

LEFT At Buitenverwachting, top quality cabernet sauvignon and sauvignon blanc are made by winemaker Herman Kirschbaum, who firmly believes that this is the right territory for Bordeaux-style varietals.

Neighboring Klein Constantia was also once part of Van der Stel's legacy, but the similarity ends there, for this is a family venture, resurrected in the 1980s from a 50-year winemaking hiatus by father-and-son team Duggie and Lowell Jooste. Winemaker, gregarious Ross Gower, matches New World richness with Old World elegance in the signature Marlbrook Bordeaux blend and a wonderfully rich sauvignon blanc. But it is the Vin de Constance that captivates; for this wood-matured naturally sweet (non-botrytis) dessert wine is made in memory of the legendary 18th-century Constantia wines that once took the world by storm.

Buitenverwachting, another classic Cape estate, has a gabled homestead that dates from 1796. Despite its hard to pronounce name, which means 'beyond expectation', Buitenverwachting's elegant wines sell like

hotcakes, which tends to leave the tasting room understocked, so order them with your meal at the gourmet restaurant or with a pre-booked picnic under the ancient oak trees.

Constantia Uitsig is a three-centuries-old farm on the edge of the valley. Chardonnay and semillon lead the way here. The wines are made off-site, but a new cellar is planned.

Nearby Steenberg is the new kid on the block. Established in the early 1990s, the state-of-the-art cellar and newly planted vineyards produce wonderfully fruity merlot and cabernet sauvignon and concentrated sauvignon blancs. The 18th-century manor house forms the core of a luxury golf estate.

Constantia's rich heritage lives on in that most civilized of life's pleasures: keeping a good table, from Buitenverwachting's formal French-style cuisine to the Provençal and Mediterranean influences at Constantia

Uitsig and La Colombe. At Groot Constantia, the cosy Jonkershuis offers traditional Cape-Malay dishes such as bobotie and malva pudding, while light lunches are available at the Tavern. Stylish Spaanschemat River Café gives a taste of local trendiness, and popular Parks Restaurant, just across the main highway towards Cape Town, is top-class.

There is accommodation to match all budgets, from the Relais & Châteaux Cellars-Hohenort Hotel and the elegant Alphen Hotel to numerous guesthouses and B&Bs.

During the summer, enquire about jazz concerts at Buitenverwachting, the antiques and collectables fair at Groot Constantia every weekend, and the outdoor craft market held opposite Constantia Village shopping mall on the last Saturday of each month. Sunday craft markets and outdoor sunset concerts are held at Kirstenbosch Botanical

Gardens, a glorious showcase of indigenous flora, with breathtaking views from its mountain-side trails. Take your own picnic or relax at the coffee shop and restaurant.

Leaving behind the manor houses and ancient oaks of Constantia, head southeast via the busy N2 where an hour's drive takes you up the sweeping Sir Lowry's Pass, on the opposite side of False Bay, and into the Hottentots-Holland mountains, where the cool-climate region of Elgin lies among apple orchards and pine tree plantations. Just past the massive apple packing sheds of the Kromco co-op, turn left to Paul Cluver, a boutique winery where not even 10,000 cases of wine are made, including a flinty sauvignon blanc, delicately fruity pinot noir and a minerally cabernet sauvignon. African art, sculpture, and handwoven wool carpets are on sale in the tasting room. Time your visit in the summer months to coincide with a sunset concert in a forest amphitheater.

Nearby roadside farmstalls, most with adjoining restaurants, offer fresh fruit, farm cheeses, preserves, freshly baked breads and pastries, olive oils, and balsamic vinegars. Try sticky Cape brandy tart or delicate milktart instead of scones or muffins with English tea or Kenyan coffee at The Orchard or Houw Hoek farmstalls. The former has a small wine tasting and sales center for wines from the Overberg (which means 'over the mountain'). This region is all wheatfields flecked with flocks of sheep, and the rolling farmland is home to South Africa's national bird, the endangered blue crane, which you may be lucky enough to spot from the road.

Another 20 minutes' drive brings you to Beaumont in the little town of Bot River. Here, at Compagnes Drift, a colonial outpost in the 1750s, fruit farmer Raoul and his artist wife Jayne Beaumont resurrected an early 1900s cellar and reconditioned old wine-making equipment, which suits the traditional style of winemaker Niels Verburg. His wines are big and rustic: a signature oaked pinotage, barrel-treated chenin blanc, and toasty chardonnay. The warmer, drier climate and stonier soils also hold promise for typical Rhône varieties shiraz and grenache, as well as mouvèdre, which they are pioneering in their corner of the Walker Bay area. Either Jayne or Niels, and some large hounds, are usually on hand to greet visitors. Jayne will recount some wonderful stories from the old days on this Cape farm, which you can relive in the two self-catering cottages in a restored mill and outbuilding.

The heart of the Walker Bay winelands lies another 20 minutes' drive towards the coastal town of Hermanus, a once-quaint fishing village that is now one of the Cape's favorite holiday spots and a popular retirement destination. At the town's entrance lies the Hemel-en-Aarde valley ('heaven and earth') which, like Constantia, enjoys a cool, maritime climate. The lean, stony, shale-derived soils, virgin viticultural territory until just over two decades ago, give

OPPOSITE Constantia's vineyards, on south-facing slopes overlooking False Bay, enjoy a cool maritime climate, ideal for slow-ripening and full flavors.
RIGHT Bouchard Finlayson, in the Hemel-en-Aarde valley, follows the Burgundian way of close planting in five-row blocks to help contain grape yields.

the valley's wines a distinctiveness that is almost obsessively strived for at Hamilton Russell Vineyards (HRV) and Bouchard Finlayson, both of which look to Burgundy for inspiration. Anthony Hamilton Russell, his affable winemaker Kevin Grant, and neighbor Peter Finlayson, specialize in classic, elegant, French-oak matured pinot noirs and chardonnays. Their approach is cerebral and intellectual, with consideration marking everything from specific vineyard site selection, planting methods, yeast and clonal variation to using different bottlings of the same variety to highlight intrinsic style differences. These are among South Africa's highest priced and most renowned wines, and are often in short supply.

Visits to Hamilton Russell and Bouchard Finlayson offer more than just wine tasting. HRV makes its own cold-pressed extra virgin olive oil and estate-matured cheeses. Anthony's wife, internationally schooled artist Arabella Caccia, creates massive abstract oils in her chapel-like mountaintop studio, with viewings by appointment. Also by appointment, fervent nature lover Peter Finlayson will guide visitors on trails through the indigenous *fynbos* vegetation.

Steely sauvignon blanc, fleshed out with tropical fruit, comes into its own in Walker Bay and is bottled by most of the cellars. The variety is synonymous with passionate winemaker and keen crayfish diver Bartho Eksteen, who in addition to making his own wines, consults for new Hemel-en-Aarde cellar Sumaridge; and fellow diver and angler Dave Johnson. The latter's easy-drinking sauvignon blanc, chardonnay, and cabernet/merlot blends made at his hilltop winery, Newton Johnson, vie for attention with stunning views across the valley to the sea.

Take time to explore the origins of two local labels: Hamilton Russell's Southern Right and WhaleHaven, under which winemaker Storm Kreusch bottles excellent pinot noir and very drinkable merlot, cabernet sauvignon and shiraz. The walls of the Old Harbor at Hermanus and the rocks at tiny De Kelders, on the opposite end of the wide, arcing Walker Bay, offer incredible sightings of mating and calving Southern Right whales, particularly in the spring months from August to November. Stay over at the exclusive Marine Hotel (a stablemate of Constantia's Cellars-Hohenort) and you might hear their rumblings and blowings from your room, or from the smart Pavilion Restaurant which overlooks the Old Harbor.

Enjoy an alfresco lunch at the Burgundy Restaurant or head down the cliffs to the informal Bientang's Cave at the water's edge. Match Walker Bay wines with seafoods such as crayfish (Cape rock lobster), black mussels, abalone (*perlemoen*), and freshly caught line fish such as *kingklip*, *galjoen* and *snoek*.

At Wine & Co., in the seafront Village Square, Bartho Eksteen's wife Suné sells all the local labels, plus a selection of other Cape and imported wines and a wide range of farm cheeses. The many interesting arts, crafts, old Cape furniture and book shops include the quaint, yet excellently stocked, Book Cottage. The Wine Village at the entrance to the Hemel-en-Aarde Valley offers daily tastings of Cape wines.

Return to Cape Town via the scenic coastal road which meanders through the villages of Kleinmond, Betty's Bay and Gordon's Bay and is renowned for its rugged mountain scenery, scented indigenous *fynbos* vegetation and sweeping sea views. The direct route, via the N2 and Sir Lowry's Pass, should take about two hours, but allow more time if you choose the coastal road.

BELOW The tasting room at Hamilton Russell Vineyards; capturing the essence of the local terroir is a hallmark of their distinctive, high-priced wines.

CONSTANTIA, ELGIN AND WALKER BAY

MAIN GRAPES
Red: Cabernet sauvignon, pinot noir, shiraz, merlot, pinotage.
White: Sauvignon blanc, chardonnay, Rhine (weisser) riesling, sémillon.

LEADING AREAS AND PRODUCERS
Constantia: Buitenverwachting, Constantia Uitsig, Groot Constantia, Klein Constantia, Steenberg.
Elgin/Overberg: Beaumont, Paul Cluver.
Walker Bay: Bartho Eksteen, Bouchard Finlayson, Hamilton Russell Vineyards, Newton Johnson, WhaleHaven.

MAIN TOWNS
Cape Town, Constantia, Grabouw/Elgin, Bot River, Hermanus.

AIRPORTS
Cape Town.

DAYS
Three.

BEST TIME TO GO
October to April. (Whale watching: August to November.)

SUMMARY
Constantia – Elgin – Bot River – Hermanus – Kleinmond – Gordon's Bay – Cape Town.

SOURCES OF INFORMATION
• *Constantia Wine Route*
Tel: +27 (21) 794-1810, Fax: +27 (21) 794-1812.
E-mail: wine@icon.co.za
• *Hermanus Tourism Bureau*
Tel: +27 (28) 312-2629, Fax: +27 (28) 313-0305.
E-mail: infoburo@intec.co.za

ABOVE At the tiny, rustic Beaumont cellar, the no-nonsense team offers visitors a real working wine farm experience with a personal touch. Bed and breakfast cottages are also available for those who want to stay over.
CENTER Although minimalist, Klein Constantia's tasting room is regularly voted the friendliest in the Cape.
RIGHT The cliffs at Walker Bay offer some of the best land-based whale watching in the world.

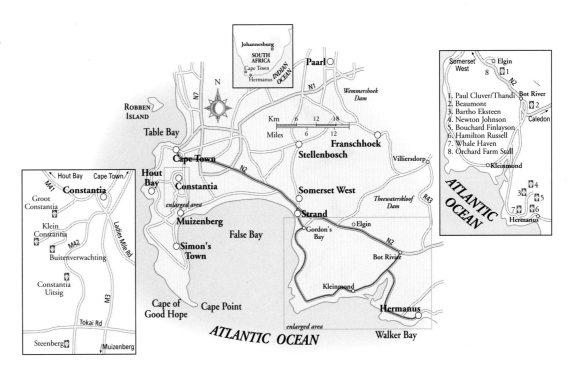

CHILE

CHRISTINE AUSTIN

A journey to the vineyards of Chile is like no other in the world. With its snow-capped Andes, pebble-strewn rivers, rich green vineyards and, if you are lucky, a pair of condors circling lazily in the sky – the total effect is breathtaking.

We are used to thinking that Chilean wines are relatively new on the world market, but the country has been growing grapes and making wine for centuries. Spanish conquistadors brought the first vines to this land in the 16th century and they thrived in Chile's fertile soil. A few centuries later, the quality of Chilean wine received a boost when new cuttings, mainly cabernet sauvignon and merlot, were imported directly from Bordeaux.

The 1980s saw a revival in the industry, with major new investment pouring into the wineries. Shining stainless steel began to replace old wooden fermentation vats, and a new wine style emerged with fresher fruit and deeper flavors. Now attention has moved to the vineyards, which in the past were planted only on flat valley floors so that they could be flooded with irrigation water. Massive irrigation systems have been put in place to deliver exactly the right amount of water to each vine, drop by drop. This means that vineyards can now be planted on slopes where the more challenging growing conditions produce more exciting wines.

Chile has an excellent climate for vines. Most wine grapes are grown in an area stretching from about 60 miles (100 kilometers) north of the capital, Santiago, to about 250 miles (400 kilometers) south. They are concentrated in an arable valley between the majestic Andes, which form Chile's eastern border, and the small rounded hills along the long western coastline. Cutting across this central valley are secondary valleys – Maipo, Rapel, Curicó and Maule – each with its own river, soil type, and microclimate, giving a particular character to their wines.

LEFT Sunset over La Palmería vineyard in the Cachapoal Valley. The vineyard is named after the ancient palm trees which grow amongst the vines.

ABOVE Gradually, Chile's wineries are opening up to tourists – and signs like this graphically lead the way! Veramonte's vineyards, which produce red and white grapes, are in a sheltered part of the Casablanca Valley.

OPPOSITE The Don Maximiano vineyard at Errazuriz in the Aconcagua Valley was one of the first in Chile to be planted on the cooler slopes, for in this region, temperatures easily reach 86°F (30°C) and above.

Rain falls only in winter. For the rest of the year the climate is dry and, because of this, Chile has few pests and diseases, so spraying against them is minimal. Chile's isolated location behind the Andes and against the sea means that it is also free from phylloxera, the pest which devastated the vineyards of France in the late 19th century and eventually swept through most of the world's vineyards. This means that Chile's vines can grow on their own roots, a huge advantage over grafted vines. Furthermore, many of the original vine cuttings were imported during the 19th century, before the onset of phylloxera in France. Carmenère, a full-flavored variety long gone from French vineyards, is still thriving here, adding its own particular flavor to the wines.

Wine tourism is relatively new in Chile, particularly outside Santiago. Most wineries are happy to receive those who plan ahead and arrange appointments in advance, but only a few have facilities to welcome visitors without an appointment. The Chileans are naturally hospitable though, and proud of their achievements, so with a little planning beforehand, they will make every effort to be as welcoming as possible.

Any tour of Chile's vineyards should start in Santiago. Whilst urban sprawl has encroached on most of the vineyards within the city, there are still some vines to be seen around the old winery at Cousiño Macul. This lies to the southeast of the city and is a beautiful old estate. Continuing in the same direction, stop at Pirque to explore the old bodega (cellar) and attractive gardens of Chile's largest wine producer, Concha y Toro. Most of the production for this company is now in cellars closer to the vineyards, but this historic bodega echoes back 100 years to how things were done in the past.

Whilst any view of the past is interesting, the vineyards and wine regions of Chile have moved on substantially in recent decades. The best way to see this progress is to visit the Casablanca Valley, one of the country's newest wine regions. Situated 50 miles (80 kilometers) northwest of Santiago, it lies behind a range of shrubby hills which are a source of lapis lazuli, the blue precious stone sold in the shops of Santiago. Beyond these hills, the land slopes down towards the Pacific Ocean, where the cool sea breezes and mists keep temperatures down and provide one of the best places to grow white grapes.

Many companies have vineyards here, but only a few actually make wine in the valley. Of these, Veramonte is certainly the most impressive and it is open to visitors.

Further down the valley, Casas del Bosque has built a new winery and there are plans to open up to visitors when it is complete. The drive through the Casablanca Valley is spectacular, with vineyards spread out across the valley floor and on the lower slopes of the hills. The road leads directly to Valparaíso, the main port of Chile, and while this city is a typical busy port, you should not miss the funiculars which connect the old town to some of the best viewpoints. Further along the bay, the beach resort of Viña del Mar has excellent seafood restaurants where pink clams (*machas*), abalone (*locos*), and local white fish (*congrio*) are particular specialties.

You could return to Santiago before exploring Aconcagua, but with a good map you should be able to head north along the coast and inland along the Aconcagua River towards Panquehue, just west of San Felipe. This is the home of Errázuriz, an outstanding winery, set in a mountainous landscape. It appears much as it did 100 years ago, with a grand entrance, gardens and comfortable armchairs in the shade, but behind the old-world comfort, a bright new winery is addressing the requirements of 21st-century wine-making. Open by appointment only.

From Panquehue, head back to Santiago before tackling the vineyards to the south. The main road out of Santiago is the Pan-American highway, a truck-laden route which nevertheless provides an easy link between the capital and the vineyards of the south. Distances are deceptively large and, once off the highway, local roads can easily deteriorate into no more than sandy tracks, so allow plenty of time to reach your destination.

The Maipo Valley, the first region on the road south, is a well-established area that is home to many head offices and wineries. It is a warm, fairly dry region which excels at producing red grapes, particularly cabernet sauvignon and carmenère. Santa Rita, the oldest winery in Maipo, is situated in Buin. It is only open by appointment, but has an excellent restaurant onsite. Viña Carmen, owned by Santa Rita, is just a short walk across the adjacent vineyards.

Between Rancagua and Chimbarongo, the fertile Rapel region, fed by the Cachapoal and Tinguiririca rivers, is home to many wineries and vineyards. The scenery here is spectacular, particularly off the beaten track, and exploration is made easier by a new hotel which has opened in Santa Cruz, in the heart of the Colchagua region, from where there is the opportunity to visit wineries such as Casa Lapostolle, Luis Felipe Edwards, MontGras, Viu Manent, and Santa Laura. The local wine organization, *Viños de Colchagua*, will help arrange visits, and provide transport.

Further south, Curicó and Maule are both major vineyard regions with a number of large-scale wineries, but wine tourism still has some way to develop here.

The best time to visit Chile is during the dry summer months, between November and April, when the temperature in much of the country is warm, but not oppressive. Humidity is never high during the summer.

While in Chile there are some experiences you must not miss. The cable car ride to the summit of Cerro San Cristóbal in Santiago, pelicans swooping around the rocks at Viña del Mar, and enjoying a chardonnay as the sun goes down are just some of the highlights; or try a cool pisco sour, made with the local, and lethal, brandy. Don't go home without tasting fresh bread baked in roadside ovens and advertised by a white flag flapping in the breeze, or *empanadas* (small handmade pastries filled with ground beef), another roadside specialty.

RIGHT The ochre-toned walls and terracotta roof tiles of Luis Felipe Edwards winery blend into the surrounding rugged hills of the Colchagua Valley.

CHILE

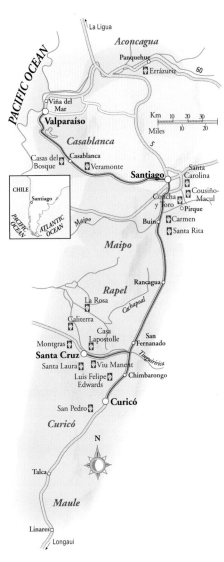

FAR LEFT At Viña Santa Rita in the Maipo Valley, the elegant old estate house is now a luxury restaurant.

LEFT Old barrels abound in historic wineries, such as here at Concha y Toro, but most new cellars are equipped with modern stainless steel.

MAIN GRAPES

Red: Cabernet sauvignon, merlot, carmenère.
White: Chardonnay, sauvignon blanc.

LEADING REGIONS AND PRODUCERS

Casablanca: Casas del Bosque, Veramonte.
Aconcagua: Viña Errázuriz.
Maipo: Concha y Toro, Santa Carolina, Santa Rita, Viña Carmen, Viña Cousiño Macul (Santiago).
Rapel: Caliterra, Casa Lapostolle, Luis Felipe Edwards (all in Colchagua); Viña La Rosa (Cachapoal).
Curicó: Montes, San Pedro.
Other regions: Maule, Itata, Bío-Bío.

MAIN TOWNS
Santiago, Valparaíso, Santa Cruz, Curicó.

AIRPORT Santiago.

DAYS Eight.

BEST TIME TO GO November to April.

SUMMARY

Santiago – Casablanca Valley – Valparaíso –
Viña del Mar – Aconcagua Valley –
Panquehue – Santiago – Buin –
Colchagua Valley (Santa Cruz).

SOURCES OF INFORMATION

• *Ruta del Vino de Colchagua*
Plaza de Armas 140, Santa Cruz,
Valle de Colchagua, Chile.
Tel: +56 (72) 823-199.
E-mail: rv@uva.cl
Web: www.colchaguavalley.cl

ARGENTINA

JIM BUDD

Argentina is one of the least known and least explored wine regions. Although it is the fifth largest wine producer in the world, the country is only now moving onto the world's wine stage. It is still early days for wine tourism, but this is an exciting time to visit as the country's wine industry is in the middle of a revolution – changing from bulk wine to quality wine production. In recent years, the industry has attracted a lot of foreign investment from America, Europe, and Australia. There is also some spectacular scenery, especially when close to the Andes.

There are over 500,000 acres (200,000 hectares) of vines planted in Argentina. In the past, the vast majority of the wine produced was of poor quality, for consumption on the thirsty home market, where over 22 gallons (100 liters) a year was drunk per head, but that has now changed, with consumption per head dropping to just under 9 gallons (40 liters). As a result, Argentina has to find new markets for its wines and also has to change to quality wines.

Most of the wine is red, with malbec the most successful variety by far. This is a powerful, robust and slightly rustic variety that is planted in southwest France, especially around Cahors. In Argentina's warmer climate, malbec gives a rounder, softer wine than in France. Increasing amounts of cabernet sauvignon, merlot, and syrah are being planted, as well as Italian varieties barbera, bonarda, and sangiovese. For the whites, torrontés, a variety indigenous to Spain's Galicia, gives perfumed wines that are reminiscent of muscat and gewürztraminer but with a touch of bitterness in the finish. Chardonnay, sauvignon blanc, and viognier are also planted.

All Argentina's vineyards are in the west, close to the Andes. Buenos Aires, although it is hundreds of miles from the country's vineyards, is the main point of entry for international air travelers. It is also the focal point for internal flights. Often it is necessary to return to Buenos Aires

LEFT A typical old-style high-trained vineyard in Maipú, Mendoza. Flood irrigation is giving way to lower trellised vines with drip-feed irrigation that gives greater control over the amount of water each vine receives.

before flying out to another region. It is not possible, for instance, to fly directly from Salta to Mendoza. Buenos Aires is an elegant and cosmopolitan city – some of its streets are reminiscent of Barcelona. It is well worth spending a day or two here, making sure that you take in a tango show one evening.

An alternative start is via Santiago in Chile, flying from there to either Mendoza or Salta or, for the adventurous, driving the 220 miles (350 kilometers) over the Andes to Mendoza (allow six hours for the journey).

The country's most northerly vineyards are at Salta and Cafayate. Salta is a two-hour flight northwest from Buenos Aires. Much of the flight is over flat plains and it is not until you are close to Salta that the terrain becomes mountainous and more interesting.

From Salta it is a three-hour drive south to Cafayate, which nestles on the edge of the Andes and is certainly one of Argentina's most beautiful wine regions. The last hour of the drive to Cafayate is through a spectacular red stone gorge with dramatically twisted rock strata, where the hills and cliffs are eroded into fantastical shapes.

Cafayate is 5553 feet (1683 meters) above sea level and some of the highest vineyards in the world are found here, with the backdrop of the Andes making them even more dramatic. During the summer months, the big difference between the high daytime temperatures (up to 104°F/40°C) and the cooler nights helps to maintain good acidity levels in the grapes, which provides flavor.

The two main wineries in Cafayate are Michel Torino, whose winery is an attractive white stuccoed building, and Etchart, which forms part of the international Pernod Ricard empire. Cafayate is a popular summer resort, so it is worth avoiding the peak time of February and early March.

Mendoza is situated 560 miles (900 kilometers) south of Cafayate. About 70 percent of Argentina's wine (and around 90 percent of its exported wine) is produced here. It takes two days to drive there, so it is preferable to return to Salta, fly to Buenos Aires and back out to Mendoza. However, the drive from Cafayate to Mendoza takes you through the wine regions of La Rioja and then

OPPOSITE A hailstorm approaching Valentin Bianchi, San Rafael. Hail poses a great danger to vines, stripping the leaves and bruising the fruit.

BELOW LEFT The very attractive Spanish-style Bodega de la Rosa is part of the property of Michel Torino, one of the main wineries in Cafayate.

BELOW RIGHT French-owned Bodegas Etchart at Cafayate is one of the highest commercial vineyards in the world, at 5400 feet (1650 meters).

San Juan, which lies just to the north of Mendoza. Neither region's wines are yet making much impact outside Argentina. There are fewer than 20 wineries in La Rioja, but in San Juan, where there are over 300 wineries, there are some significant new projects, so this situation is likely to change soon.

As in the rest of Argentina, Mendoza's vineyards have to be irrigated and are dependent on plentiful water from the Andes. Flying into Mendoza, you see how important irrigation is. A sharp line divides the bright green cultivated land from the dull desert scrub. Many of the vineyards are covered in netting as protection against hail because the area is prone to violent storms that come down off the Andes. Golf-ball-sized hailstones can destroy a crop in just a few minutes.

Mendoza is a bustling, noisy city and many of the wineries are clustered together

around it. The chief vine-growing zones of Mendoza are Maipú to the east of the city, Luján de Cuyo to the west and Tupungato, situated some 40 miles (70 kilometers) south and into the foothills of the Andes. There are considerable differences in altitude between the different zones of Mendoza. To date, Moët & Chandon's Terrazas project has been the most explicit in exploiting the climatic differences between these zones, by planting syrah in the lowest vineyards, chardonnay in the highest, and other grapes inbetween.

La Agricola is run by the dynamic José Zuccardi. Horse rides to the vineyards can be arranged in advance, with the chance of tasting the appropriate wine beside the vines: a glass of malbec, for example, beside some malbec vines. Other wineries in this area that are worth visiting include Trapiche, which is the quality arm of the very large Peñaflor

The vineyards of San Rafael are flatter and further away from the Andes than those of Mendoza. There is less chance of hail here, so few vineyards are protected with nets. On the northern outskirts of San Rafael is Valentin Bianchi, a sparkling wine producer. A sign proclaims: Bianchi – home of Champaña. Of course it isn't real champagne; that can only be made in the designated area in France. European Union protection of names has yet to reach Argentina, and wine shops still carry Argentinian beaujolais or chablis. The impressive Bianchi buildings are set in parkland and there are organized tours.

Another significant San Rafael winery is Balbi, which is owned by the multinational Allied Domecq, and whose best wines are based either on malbec or syrah.

The cool-climate Río Negro in northern Patagonia is Argentina's most southerly wine region. Once again there is no direct flight, so it is either a question of making the long drive south or returning to Buenos Aires to fly down to the Río Negro. Humberto Canale, at General Roca, is the leading producer here, with vines planted in the shelter of the valley. The slow, cool ripening conditions help to intensify the flavor of the grapes.

Throughout the country, beef is the staple diet; hardly surprising as Argentina is a major producer. The quality of the meat is very high and barbecuing is the most popular form of cooking. A rich malbec goes wonderfully well with a large rare steak. Small filled pastries, *empandas*, are the most common first course. Traditionally they are cooked in a small clay oven and served immediately, so heat-resistant fingers are an advantage! The filling is often minced beef but cheese is a popular alternative.

group, apparently the world's third largest wine company, and Norton, which produces the most consistent range of wines in Argentina (their malbec is particularly good).

In 2001, Nicolas Cateña opened at Agrelo in Luján de Cuyo. Architecturally, his ultra-modern Cateña Zapata winery is clearly inspired by the ancient Egyptians. By contrast, Bodega Lopez is an interesting example of a traditional winery that produces some good wines, albeit in an older style.

It is a little over a two-hour drive down to San Rafael from Mendoza and en route, you could make a detour to Tupungato to visit the Salentein winery. Unfortunately the wines are currently not quite as impressive as the winery design but that may well change, as the venture is very new. After the town of Pareditas, the last hour to San Rafael is through an empty landscape with no sign of habitation for 60 miles (100 kilometers), a reminder of just how vast this country is.

ARGENTINA

MAIN GRAPES

Red: Malbec, merlot, cabernet sauvignon, barbera, bonarda.
White: Chardonnay, torrontes.

LEADING REGIONS AND PRODUCERS

Cafayate: Etchart, Michel Torino.
Mendoza: Cateña, La Agricola, Lopez, Norton, Terrazas (Moët & Chandon), Trapiche (Peñaflor).
San Rafael: Bianchi, Balbi.
Río Negro: Humberto Canale.

MAIN TOWNS AND AIRPORTS

Buenos Aires, Mendoza, Salta, San Rafael. (Santiago in Chile is an alternative.)

DAYS One or preferably two weeks.

BEST TIME TO GO September to November.

SUMMARY Buenos Aires – Salta – Cafayate – Mendoza – San Rafael – Río Negro.

SOURCES OF INFORMATION

Wines of Argentina
Buenos Aires:
Guemes Giordano 4464,
CP 1425 Buenos Aires, Argentina.
Tel: +54 (11) 4776-2529
Fax: +54 (11) 4774-4873.
Web: www.bodegasdeargentina.com
London:
Imperial Studios, 3 Imperial Road,
Fulham SW6 2AG, United Kingdom.
Tel: + 44 (20) 7751-9170
Fax: +44 (20) 7610-6007.
Email: WinesofArgentina@westbury.co.uk

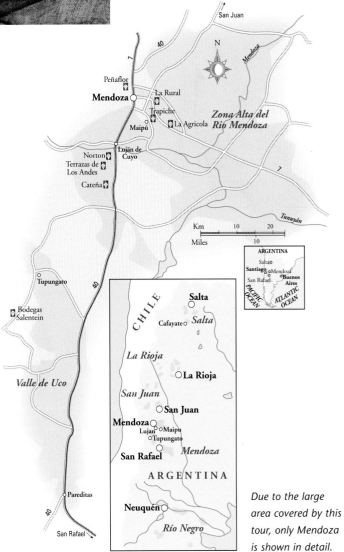

Due to the large area covered by this tour, only Mendoza is shown in detail.

CONTRIBUTORS

CHRISTINE AUSTIN (Chile) has traveled extensively within the world of wine, visiting vineyards and taking photographs for articles for a variety of publications, including *Decanter* and *Wine*. She has spent several weeks in Chile, most recently in 2001. Her books include two editions of the *Which? Wine Guide* and she is a wine consultant to *Larousse Gastronomique*. She lectures and broadcasts regularly on wine for radio and has also appeared on television.

STEPHEN BROOK (Burgundy, Napa, Sonoma) became a full-time writer in 1982, initially specializing in travel books, notably *New York Days, New York Nights* and *The Double Eagle*. He has written 30 books, including the prize-winning *The Wines of California*, and *Bordeaux: People, Power and Politics*, which was shortlisted for the 2002 Andre Simon Award. A contributing editor of *Decanter* and a frequent contributor to other magazines and newspapers, he is currently completing a book on the wines of Germany.

PETER FORRESTAL (Margaret River, McLaren Vale) is a freelance wine writer, based in Perth, Western Australia, and the associate editor of *Australian Gourmet Traveller Wine*. He is author, co-author or editor of 23 books including the *Global Encyclopedia of Wine; Discover Australia: Wineries; A Taste of the Margaret River*, and the annual New Holland publication *Quaff: Best wines in Australia under $15* (with Max Allen). He is also the editor of the *Oxford Companion to the Wines of Australia and New Zealand*.

ROSEMARY GEORGE MW (Languedoc, Marlborough) was lured into the wine trade by a glass of the Wine Society's champagne nearly 30 years ago and was one of the first women to become a Master of Wine. A freelance wine writer since 1981, her nine books include *The Wines of New Zealand* and *The Wines of the South of France, From Banyuls to Bellet*.

PATRICIA GUY (Tuscany, Veneto) has worked in New York, London and Paris, as well as in Champagne, Bordeaux and the Midi as a fine wine broker and wine buyer, *vendangeuse*, sommelier, tasting tutor, marketing and public relations director. Following studies in wine tasting, viticulture and oenology in London, she

won the Wine Spectator Scholarship and the International Vintners Scholarship. She lives in Verona and writes about Italian wines, spirits and restaurants for a variety of English and American magazines. Her books include *Amarone: Verona's Great Red Wine; Gusto!, a guide to Italian grape varieties*, and *Bacchus at Baker Street*.

LINDA JOHNSON-BELL (Alsace) is an award-winning international wine journalist, author and wine jury member. She contributes regularly to both *Wine* (UK) and *Decanter* magazines' tasting panels. She is the author of *The Home Cellar Guide* and *Good Food Fine Wine* and was the UK editor of *Vintage* magazine in Paris, where she lived for over 10 years (much of it spent sipping in Alsace). She is a member of the Circle of Wine Writers and the Society of Authors and is a committee member of FIJEV (La Fèdèration Internationale des Journalistes et Ecrivains du Vin). She lives near Oxford and in London where she is the wine buyer for her husband's restaurant/bar in Notting Hill.

JAMES LAWTHER MW (St Emilion) began his career in the wine trade retailing wine at Steven Spurrier's Paris shop, Caves de la Madeleine, and as a lecturer at the Acadèmie du Vin. In 1993 he was the first Englishman to pass the Master of Wine exam while resident in France. Based in Bordeaux, he is an independent wine consultant and writer who also leads tours to the French wine regions. He is a contributing editor to *Decanter*, author of the *Bordeaux Wine Companion* and contributed the Bordeaux section of the *Global Encyclopedia of Wine*.

JOHN LIVINGSTONE-LEARMONTH (Rhône) wrote the first book on Rhône wines, *The Wines of the Rhône* when living in Aix-en-Provence in 1974–75. He is now working on the 4th edition. John writes mainly about French wines. His articles have been published in a broad range of British magazines, from *Decanter, Wine, Harpers, Wine & Spirit* to *Good Housekeeping* and *The Connoisseur*. He is also a regular contributor to the *Singapore Wine Review*. He contributes to annuals like Hugh Johnson's *Pocket Wine Book* and Hugh Johnson's *Wine Atlas*, and has given talks in Britain, the USA and Asia. He is an honorary citizen of Châteauneuf-du-Pape.

GILES MACDONOGH (Rheingau, Mosel, Wachau) is the author of four books on wine. These include *The Wine and Food of Austria; Austria: New Wines from the Old World* and, most recently *Portuguese Table Wines*. In addition, he has written seven books on French and German history, including histories of Berlin and Prussia and biographies of Frederick the Great and the last Kaiser. He is a regular contributor to the *Financial Times* and *Punch* and also writes for Williams-Sonoma *Taste* in the USA.

JOHN RADFORD (Jerez, Rioja-Navarra) writes for specialist and trade magazines in the UK and has recently contributed articles on Spain and Portugal to the *Global Encyclopedia of Wine* and *A Century of Wine*. His book *The New Spain* won four international awards in 1999–2000 and a new edition is planned for 2004. He co-wrote, with Stephen Brook, the Mitchell Beazley *Pocket Guide to Fortified and Sweet Wines* and has compiled and edited the Spanish Wine Education Notes since 1989; the 2002 edition is to be published on the Internet.

WENDY TOERIEN (Constantia, Stellenbosch), a freelance wine writer and author, has been writing about wine since 1989 and was news editor and feature writer for *Wine Magazine* (South Africa) from its inception in 1993 to 1999. She has contributed articles on Cape wine for the *Rough Guide to South Africa* and *Insight Guide to South Africa*. She has written two books, *South African Wine: A Celebration* and *Wines and Vineyards of South Africa*, both by New Holland.

HILARY HADLEY-WRIGHT (Washington, Oregon) is a freelance writer specializing in wine, food and travel. She has written three books about wine tourism including the award-winning *Water Into Wine*, which describes a wine-lover's cruise through the vineyards of France. Her most recent book is *The Great Organic Wine Guide*. She also writes for national newspapers, magazines and websites in the UK and USA.

JIM BUDD (Loire, Douro, Argentina) also contributed the general introduction and the introductions to both the Old and New World sections, in addition to serving as the general editor of the book.

INDEX

PHOTOGRAPHIC CREDITS

Copyright rests with the following photographers and/or their agents:

Mick Rock/Cephas Picture Library photographers:

MR	=	Mick Rock
NB	=	Nigel Blythe
SB	=	Stuart Boreham
AC	=	Andy Christodolo
BF	=	Bruce Fleming
KJ	=	Kevin Judd
HL	=	Herbert Lehman
DM	=	Diana Mewes
SM	=	Steven Morris
CN	=	Charlie Napasnapper
NP	=	Neil Philips
RS	=	Roy Stedall
TS	=	Ted Stefanski
PS	=	Peter Stovell
DV	=	Daniel Valla
WM	=	Wine Magazine (UK)

Other photographers:

JP	=	Janet Price
PO	=	Portland Oregon Visitors Association
AM	=	Antonio Moya
LvH	=	Lanz van Horsten
SA	=	Struik Image Library (Shaen Adey)
Ryno	=	Struik Image Library (Ryno Reineke)

Key to locations: t = top; tl = top left; tc = top center; tr = top right; b = bottom; bl = bottom left; bc = bottom center; br = bottom right; l = left; r = right; c = center

Endpapers	MR	29	tl & tr	MR	65	tc, tr	JP	101		MR	135	KJ
1	MR	30-32		MR	65	tl	NB	102-103		JP	136-137	AC
2-3	BF	33	l	MR	66-71		JP	104		KJ	138-139	KJ
4-5	MR	33	r	SB	72-74		MR	106-107		CN	140	AC
6-7	JP	34	r	SB	75	t	HL	108		JP	141	KJ
8-9	AM	34	b	JP	75	b	WM	109		MR	142-145	LvH
10	MR	35	l	MR	76-79		MR	110		BF	146	SA
11	l	KJ	35	r	DV	80-81		AC	111	l	MR	147-149	LvH
11	r	TS	36-45		MR	82		MR	111	r	BF	150	SA
12-15	MR	46-50		JP	83	tl	HL	112-113		KJ	151-152	LvH
16	NB	51		MR	83	tc	PS	114	t	BF	153	tl, tc	LvH
18-19	MR	52		JP	83	tr	MR	114	b	TS	153	tr	SA
20	l	MR	53-55		MR	84-85		JP	115-117		TS	154-158	AC
20	r	JP	56	r	NB	86-87		MR	118-120		MR	159	l	JP
21-22	JP	56	l	JP	88		JP	121-122		MR	159	r	AC
23	tl & tc	MR	57		NB	89-91		MR	123		PO	160-161	AC
23	tr	JP	58		MR	92	l	RS	124-129		MR	162	JP
24-25	MR	59	l, r	JP	92	r	MR	130-131		KJ	163-165	AC
26	JP	60-61		MR	93		MR	132	r	JP	166	Ryno
27	DM	62	l	NB	94		NP	132	l	AC		
28	t	JP	62	r	AC	95-99		MR	133		KJ		
28	b	NB	63-64		MR	100		JP	134		MR